LIVERPOOL'S
SHIPPING GROUPS

Ian Collard

The
History
Press

Aureol in dry dock at Liverpool.

First published in 2002 by Tempus Publishing
Reprinted 2003

Reprinted in 2010 by
The History Press
The Mill, Brimscombe Port,
Stroud, Gloucestershire, GL5 2QG
www.thehistorypress.co.uk

Reprinted 2011

British Library Cataloguing in Publication Data.
A catalogue record for this book is available from the British Library.

ISBN 978 0 7524 2374 6

Typesetting and origination by Tempus Publishing
Printed and bound in Great Britain by
Marston Book Services Limited, Didcot

Contents

Acknowledgements

I am most grateful to many people for the help given to me in the preparation of this work. Duncan Haws has kindly allowed the use of the wealth of information he has gathered together in his comprehensive collection of 'Merchant Fleets' publications. John M. Young and his publication *Shipping – Today and Yesterday* and the World Ship Society have given me help and assistance in researching various issues involving the historical background of the vessels and shipping lines included in this book.

I would also like to thank the Blue Funnel Line, the Carnival Corporation, Cunard Line, Ellerman Lines, Union Castle Line, Furness Ship Management, Shaw Savill & Albion Line, Harrison Line and the Blue Star Line.

Philosopher (1857/1,059grt) was the first Harrison ship to be named after a trade or profession.

Introduction

The history of the great shipping groups of the nineteenth century is about family dynasties, business acumen, investment, risk taking and entrepreneurial skills. It is about everything that epitomizes the Victorian age. Men of vision identified market trends and gaps in the provision of shipping services throughout the world. Capital was obtained, which enabled people to speculate on present and future need and how this was to be satisfied.

Some families, and groups of investors were involved in several projects and were responsible for initiating routes that were to develop and blossom providing them with excellent returns on their original investment.

In this period, the Industrial Revolution meant that Britain became the industrial centre of the world. This created a need for raw materials to be shipped from all continents and the carriage of finished products to the new countries rapidly developing throughout the British Empire.

Ships became more luxurious and advances in technology encouraged more people to travel. Routes were developed to transport people to places like the United States, Australia, Africa, India and South America. Migration from Europe created a large market that was satisfied by the provision of berths on the large liners that also carried rich travellers in first class surroundings.

George Holt of Lamport & Holt was the elder brother of Alfred Holt who formed the Blue Funnel line. He was an apprentice with T&J Brocklebank and joined with William Lamport in 1845. Charles Booth was a cousin of William Lamport and served his apprenticeship with Lamport & Holt before forming the Booth Line, with his brother Alfred. George Holt also worked closely with his brother Alfred Holt, who was a qualified railway engineer, on an engineering project.

Sir Owen Phillips, who later became Lord Kylsant, was chairman of the Royal Mail Line in 1903. Elder Dempster Line were taken over by them in 1910 and he acquired the shares of the Lamport & Holt Line in 1911 and paid £7 million for the shares of the White Star Line in 1927.

The increase in prosperity and the industrialization of large areas of Britain during this period brought about massive investment in port, harbour and dock facilities to cater for the needs of the ships and ship owners. Cotton, steel, engineering and chemical industries were established in various parts of the country and transport infrastructures established to meet the demand created by them.

Massive dock building programmes were undertaken at London, Liverpool, Glasgow and the other major ports to increase the facilities available, and to enable the ship owners to improve the quality of service provided.

The shipping lines also invested in new, faster and more cost effective vessels to compete in what was a very aggressive international business. More countries were recognizing the need to have a prestigious merchant fleet and to be the holder of the Blue Riband trophy for the fastest crossing of the Atlantic Ocean.

Fierce competition on the North Atlantic during the twentieth century ensured that the travelling public were given the opportunity to travel on fast, luxurious and prestigious vessels that became legends of the sea. Cunard introduced *Lusitania* and *Mauretania* followed by *Aquitania, Queen Mary, Queen Elizabeth* and *Queen Elizabeth 2*.

Developments in the design of cargo liners took place as new classes of vessels were introduced to cater for the changing needs of the market. Some lines were responsible for specific cargo transportation and provided the customers with vessels designed to cater for particular needs such as refrigerated goods, oil, iron ore, chemicals or general cargo.

The container revolution of the 1960s meant that all of the established shipping groups were forced to look at the ships in their fleets and invest in new specialist container vessels and facilities. The vast expense involved meant that many of the lines were combined into large consortiums and the conventional vessels in the fleets were sold for further trading or to the ship-breakers.

Some of the established shipping lines that had been in business since Victorian times did not survive and many of the names in this book are now a memory of a different age. Others have been taken over by larger groups and their names have gradually vanished from the shipping records as their ships have been replaced or renamed.

The shipping lines shown in this book were responsible for the development of international trade across the oceans and a source of employment for many people across the world. They brought many different cultures closer together and helped to foster a greater understanding between nations, while providing income and profit for their shareholders.

They provided me with an interest that has given me so much pleasure and enjoyment over the last forty years. It was difficult to imagine in the 1960s that the shipping scene would change so dramatically in such a relatively short period. I cycled around the Birkenhead and Liverpool Dock system with my camera on my back recording vessels that represented the major shipping groups of the world. This book is a celebration of a period that will not be forgotten by anyone with an interest in ships and the sea.

One

Cunard Line

Britannia sailed from Liverpool on her maiden voyage on 4 July 1840.

Persia, the first iron-built mail Cunarder carried a spread of canvas and retained the clipper bow that was not discarded until the *Abyssinia* of 1870.

In 1839 Samuel Cunard was introduced to Robert Napier, an experienced engineer, George Burns and David MacIver, ship owners in the British coastal trade and a contract was signed between the Lords of the Admiralty to provide a transatlantic mail service. The departure of the wooden paddle steamer *Britannia* from Liverpool on 4 July 1840 marked the beginning of a great adventure by Cunard who had arrived in England from Canada in 1839. He and his brothers had been involved in various shipping operations including managing the agency for the East India Company. *Britannia* took fourteen days, eight hours to reach New York on her maiden voyage.

Arcadia, *Caledonia*, *Columbia* were joined by *Hibernia* in 1843 and *Cambria* replaced *Columbia* the following year. Navigation Acts were repealed in 1849 which enabled goods from Europe to be transhipped via Britain to America or the Mediterranean. Charles MacIver started a shipping service to the Levant and in 1851 Samuel Cunard became involved in the company. Eleven Cunard vessels were taken over in 1854 to transport troops to the Crimean War and this had a serious effect on their ability to provide the mail service to America. They were chartered at £2.50 per ton per month to carry troops and stores to Scutari and Balaclava.

The British & Foreign Steam Navigation Co. was formed in 1855 to provide services to ports in the Mediterranean with the vessels *Alps*, *Andes*, *British Queen*, *Damascus*, *Lebanon*, *Karnak*, *Teneriffe* and *Taurus*. This service enabled many of the smaller Atlantic ships to be retained and placed in the Mediterranean service. *Andes* was the first Cunarder to be built of iron, and the first to be propeller driven. She was slightly larger than *Britannia* and carried two classes of passengers. *Persia* was introduced in 1856 and was the largest ship in the world at the time of her launch. As she was 119 metres she was nearly twice the length of the *Britannia*. At 3,300 gross tons she was three times bigger than *Britannia* and compared to *Britannia* of 740hp she was 3,600 horse power with a speed of $12\frac{1}{2}$ knots and her paddle wheels were forty feet in diameter. In 1862 the last paddle-driven Cunard steamer, *Scotia*, was completed and the delivery of the first screw-propelled mail ship *China* of 2,550 gross tons took place.

The American Civil War affected passenger numbers during the 1860s. In 1865 the war ended and the completion of the Atlantic telegraph enabled the news of Samuel Cunard's death to be reported on 28 April. Thomas Henry Ismay provided competition to the Cunard Line with the introduction of the White Star Line vessels *Atlantic*, *Baltic*, *Oceanic* and *Republic* in 1871, and Cunard introduced *Bothnia* and *Scythia* in 1874.

On 21 May 1878 the Cunard Steam Ship Co. was formed and the 17 knot, steel-hulled *Servia* was introduced in 1881. *Servia* was the first Cunarder to be fitted with electric lighting. She was joined by *Aurania* the following year and in 1883 the Line took over the Guion Liner, *Oregon*, and regained the Blue Riband of the Atlantic. *Umbria* and *Etruria*, introduced in 1884, had accommodation for 550 first class passengers and 500 steerage. Their compound machinery developed 14,000hp and they were among the highest powered single-screw steamers ever built. The *Umbria* achieved a speed of 20.18 knots on trails and *Etruria* was slightly faster.

The first twin-screw steamers, *Campania* and *Lucania*, were introduced in 1893. They had a daily coal consumption of 480 tons and each vessel was capable of a speed of over 21 knots. They were the fastest Atlantic liners at the time and in 1901 Marconi carried out his early experiments in wireless transmission on board. Between 1895 and 1905 fifteen new vessels were introduced with a combined gross tonnage of 138,600 tons.

The beginning of the twentieth century saw Cunard looking at new ideas of machinery and propulsion. *Caronia* was introduced in 1905 with quadruple expansion engines and *Carmania* was installed with high-powered steam turbines which made her one and a half knots faster than her sister ship. The turbines developed over 18,000hp giving her a speed of 21 knots on trails enabling Cunard to consider this type of propulsion for two vessels *Mauretainia* and *Lusitania*, which were being planned at this time.

These two ships were to be the largest and fastest of their type. On her second voyage in 1907 *Lusitania* took the Blue Riband record with an average speed of 24 knots. *Mauretania* followed her into service and on her return homeward maiden voyage she beat *Lusitania*'s time by twenty-one minutes by completing the voyage in four days, twenty-two hours and twenty-nine minutes. *Mauretania* became one of Cunard Line's most famous ships and for more than

Etruria, one of the record breakers of the 1880s, showed the way to the famous *Campania* and *Lucania* of the next decade.

Campania was the first twin-screw Cunarder and an Atlantic record holder within a year of her completion.

twenty-two years she was the fastest liner on the North Atlantic. For twenty-seven consecutive voyages she averaged a speed of 25½ knots.

The Boston route saw the commissioning of *Franconia* in 1911 and *Laconia* in 1912 and the Thompson Line was purchased to strengthen the Canadian routes and Anchor Line (Henderson Brothers) was taken over.

On 31 May 1914 *Aquitania* sailed on her maiden voyage and with *Caronia* and *Carmania* she was taken over by the Admiralty and they were converted into Armed Merchant Cruisers. *Lusitania* was torpedoed, and sank in under twenty minutes off the Old Head of Kinsale by U-20 on 7 May 1915 with a loss of 1,198 lives. In 1916 the Commonweath & Dominion Line, which later became Port Line was in-corporated with the Cunard Steam Ship Co. and their ships were given Cunard funnel colours. In 1925, the line's first motorships, *Port Dunedin* and *Port Hobart*, were delivered and they worked closely with the New Zealand Shipping Co. and Shaw Savill & Albion Line on services to New Zealand. From 1927 the Port Line was responsible for transporting the steel work for the construction of the Sydney Harbour Bridge.

At the end of the war in 1918 Cunard ordered thirteen new ships to replace the twenty-two that they had lost by enemy action. *Mauretania* and *Aquitania* were converted to burn oil fuel instead of coal. Between 1920 and 1925 the Line took delivery of thirteen new ships, including six 14,000 ton vessels for the Canadian service and five 20,000 ships for the American routes. The former German liner *Imperator* was taken over by the Company after the War and she was renamed *Berengaria*.

A share in the Brocklebank Line was obtained by the Cunard Steamship Co. in 1919 with a complete takeover not occurring until 1940. The Brocklebank Line provided a service from South Wales, Glasgow and Birkenhead to Calcutta and following acquisition by Cunard a new service from Calcutta to the East Coast of America was added to their traditional operations.

The express liner service to New York was transferred from Liverpool to Southampton in 1919 and was operated by the *Mauretania*, *Aquitania* and *Berengaria*. One of the later consequences of this move was that the two 'Queens' never actually sailed into their port of registry of Liverpool throughout their life. It was during the 1920s that the vision of a weekly two ship express service was discussed by the Cunard Line and in 1930 the keel of hull number 534 was laid at John Brown's Shipyard on the River Clyde.

However, in 1931 the world economic depression caused work on the hull to be suspended and it did not start again until the Government advanced £3 million to the Company in 1933. This grant was conditional on the merging of Cunard and the White Star Line that took place in 1934. The motorships *Britannic* and *Georgic*, built in 1930 and 1932, were the newest White Star Line vessels included in the merger. They both retained their names and White Star colours throughout their careers.

Queen Mary sailed on her maiden voyage on 27 May 1936 and work was started on her sister ship at the same slipway at John Brown's yard. *Mauretania* was launched by Lady Bates at Cammell Laird's yard at Birkenhead in 1938 and, at the time of her launch, she was the largest liner to be built in England.

In August 1938 the *Queen Mary* crossed from Bishop Rock to Ambrose Light in three days, twenty-one hours and forty-eight minutes at an average speed of 30.99 knots. A month later the *Queen Elizabeth* was launched and, when war was declared on 3 September 1939, she was sent to join her sister in New York. The Line started the war with eighteen passenger ships totalling 434,689 gross tons. Five of these were lost by enemy action, four were taken over by the Admiralty as depot ships and one was refitted as a Government troop transport.

The 'Queens' were taken over for trooping in March 1940 with *Aquitania* and *Mauretania*. *Britannic, Franconia, Georgic, Laconia, Lancastria, Samaria* and *Scythia* were also converted to troopships and the A-class ships, *Carinthia* and *Laurentic*, served as Armed Merchant Cruisers. In 1942 the *Queen Mary* collided with the cruiser that was escorting her, which sank with a loss of over 300 of her crew.

Aquitania, one of the greatest British liners, was in commission for thirty-five years. She made 442 voyages, steamed 3 million miles and carried nearly 1.2 million passengers.

Scythia sailed on her maiden voyage from Liverpool to New York on 20 August 1921. She became a troopship in 1939 and was severely damaged at Algiers in 1942. She was repaired and in 1946 she brought 2,500 German prisoners of war back from Canada. Refitted in 1949, she served Cunard until 1958 when she was broken up at Inverkeithing.

At the end of the war Cunard passenger liners had carried over 4,400,000 passengers and had steamed 5,360,000 miles. The two 'Queens' carried over a million and a half passengers as troop carriers and it was suggested that they shortened the length of the war. Six ships were lost to enemy action and four were converted to heavy repair ships for the Royal Navy.

The fleet replacement programme commenced in 1946 and *Media* sailed on her maiden voyage from Liverpool to New York on 20 August 1947. *Brescia* was added to the fleet that year and *Parthia* followed in 1948. *Caronia* was designed exclusively for cruising and her introduction in 1949 marked a significant addition to the fleet.

The sisters *Saxonia*, *Ivernia*, *Carinthia* and *Sylvania* were built for the Canadian routes in the 1950s, but with poor passenger numbers in the early 1960s the Company decided to convert *Saxonia* and *Ivernia* to cruise ships in 1963. *Saxonia* was renamed *Carmania*, *Ivernia* became *Franconia* and *Sylvania* was transferred to the Liverpool to New York service. *Mauretania* was withdrawn and sold to the ship-breakers in 1965, the year that the Company made a loss of £1.5 million on its passenger services.

The keel of a new liner was laid on 5 July 1965 at John Brown's Shipyard on the River Clyde. She was launched in 1967 by Her Majesty the Queen who named her *Queen Elizabeth 2*. Following turbine problems on her trails she finally sailed on her maiden voyage from Southampton to New York on 2 May 1969.

In an attempt to address the changing nature of the industry, especially the introduction of containerization, the Cunard Line took a 20% share in the Atlantic Container Line in 1967 with partners the French Line, Holland America, Swedish America, Transatlantic A/B and Wallenius. Through Port Line, they also became a member of Associated Container Transportation Ltd in 1969. The famous Head Office in the Cunard Building in Liverpool was sold and the Line moved its operations to London. *Queen Mary* sailed on her final voyage from New York on 22 September 1967. She left Southampton on 31 October for Long Beach in California where she had been bought by the city.

Franconia was built by John Brown & Co. in 1923. She carried out a number of cruises from New York and her world cruise in 1938 covered thirty-seven ports and 41,727 miles. She was converted to a troopship in 1939, operating to Malta, Norway, France, Suez, Madagascar and Sicily. *Franconia* returned to the Liverpool–Canada service in 1949 and was scrapped at Inverkeithing in 1956.

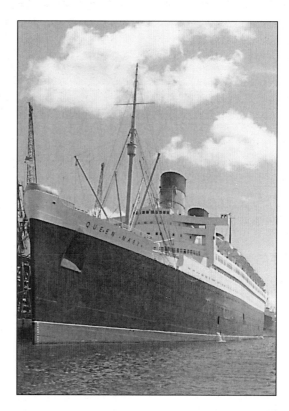

Queen Mary (1936/81,235grt) at Southampton during the National Seamans Strike in the summer of 1966.

Cargo operations were reorganized under the name of Cunard-Brocklebank in 1968 and in an attempt to diversify the Company ordered eight bulk carriers from a shipyard in Spain.

Trafalgar House Investments made a successful bid for the Company in 1971. The fleet comprised ships of H.E. Moss & Co., Cunard-Brocklebank bulk carriers, Brocklebank and Port Line cargo vessels and ten reefers of the former Maritime Fruit Carriers. Two new cruise ships, *Cunard Adventurer* and *Cunard Ambassador*, were also introduced in 1971. *Cunard Countess* and *Cunard Conquest/Princess* joined the fleet of cruise liners in 1974 and *Cunard Ambassador* suffered a serious fire and was sold. Ten cargo ships were purchased from Maritime Fruit Carriers in 1976 for the group to diversify into that market.

The Falklands Conflict of 1982 saw the *Queen Elizabeth 2* conveying troops to the Falklands where the container vessel *Atlantic Conveyor* was set on fire and sank following an attack by Exocet missiles.

Sagafjord and *Vistafjord* became part of the fleet in 1984 retaining their original names but flying Cunard funnel colours. *Sea Goddess I* and *Sea Goddess II* were taken over in 1986. The following year all cargo operations were transferred to the Atlantic Container Line and the Ellerman Group was taken over, at a cost of £24 million, and merged with the Cunard Line operations.

The Royal Viking Line was acquired from the Klosters Group of Norway in 1994. The *Royal Viking Sun* came under Cunard ownership and their other cruise ship, *Royal Viking Queen*, was transferred to the Royal Cruise Line.

Kvaernar, an Anglo-Norwegian engineering and construction company, took over Trafalgar House in 1996 and the Cunard Line faced an uncertain future. However, in 1998 the Carnival Corporation negotiated a $500 million deal, with minority partners, to merge the line with its Seabourn luxury cruise operations. In 1999, they took total control of the company by acquiring the remaining 32% share for 3.2 million Carnival shares and $76.5 million cash, a total value of $205 million.

Carnival finalized a contract with Alstom Chantiers de l'Atlantique shipyard for the construction of the world's largest ocean liner ever constructed. At 150,000 tons, *Queen Mary 2*

Queen Elizabeth (1940/83,673grt) at Southampton.

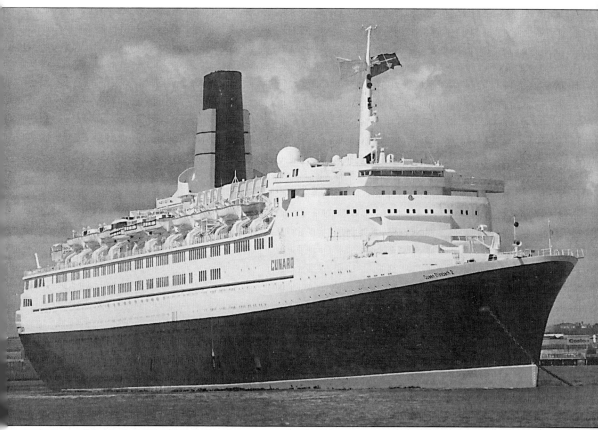

Queen Elizabeth 2 (1969/65,863grt) on a visit to the Mersey on a Round Britain cruise. She was built by John Brown on the Clyde in 1969 and was requisitioned by the British Government in 1982 to carry troops to South Georgia during the Falklands War. She returned to the Atlantic service and has since been converted from steam to diesel propulsion.

will carry 2,620 passengers, will be 345 metres long and 41 metres wide; she will have seventeen decks and will be the longest and widest passenger ship ever constructed. Costing $780 million she will enter service in 2003 and will offer the widest variety of modern facilities and amenities aboard any ocean-going vessel.

The ship will feature multiple dining venues, including the traditional grill rooms, a 1,300 seat three-deck high main restaurant and a casual poolside eatery, indoor and outdoor wraparound promenade decks, a planetarium and an art gallery exhibiting maritime paintings and memorabilia. She will have five swimming pools along with a diversity of entertainment venues, ranging from intimate to a spectacular multi deck show lounge.

Queen Mary 2 will have 1,310 staterooms, nearly three quarters of which will feature a private balcony. There will be more than ninety suites, including six penthouses offering private butler and concierge service and five duplex apartments, each featuring their own private gymnasium.

The vessel's numerous technical advancements include a state of the art MerMaid™ 'podded' propulsion system comprised two fixed and two rotating units allowing for easy manoeuvrability, along with a diesel and gas power plant capable of creating 157,000hp, which will enable the ship to sail at 30 knots.

Larry Pimentel, Cunard Line president and CEO, said that Cunard has been carrying people

Queen Mary 2 in the River Mersey in 2009.

Caronia (1973/24,492grt) was built as the *Vistafjord* and was renamed at Princes Landing Stage at Liverpool on 10 December 1999.

between Europe and America and around the world for more than 160 years. For the past six decades, there has always been a Cunard Queen on the sea. *Queen Mary 2* will be the heir to all that has gone before and she will be a showcase of the art of shipbuilding in its most refined and masterful form. *Queen Mary 2* will carry the grace and elegance of a bygone era into the future.

Including the *Queen Mary 2* project, Carnival has 16 new vessels scheduled for delivery between 2001-2006. The Carnival Corporation now comprises Carnival Cruise Lines, Holland America Line, Windstar Cruises, Cunard Line, Seabourn Cruise Line and Costa Cruises. Combined Carnival Corporation's various brands operate 48 ships in the Caribbean, Alaska, Europe and other worldwide destinations.

Early in 2002 the Carnival Corporation announced that they had signed a Letter of Intent with the Italian shipyard Fincantieri for the construcion of a new 1,968 passenger liner to serve the British market. The ship, which will cost approximately $400 million, will be delivered to Cunard in January 2005, just one year after the launch of *Queen Mary 2*. The vessel will be based at Southampton and deployed on a variety of worldwide itineraries. As Britain is now the world's second largest cruise market, Cunard Line also annouced that *Caronia* would be re-positioned to cruise out of Southampton from May 2002.

Queen Mary 2 sailed from Southampton on he rmaiden voyage to Fort Lauderdale on the 12 January 2004 carrying 2,620 passengers. She was the longest, widest and tallest passenger ship ever built and was designed as an ocean liner and cruise ship. *Caronia* was sold to Saga Shipping in 2004, becoming *Saga Ruby* following a £17 million refit in Malta.

On the 23 February 2006 *Queen Mary 2* arrived at Long Beach and exchanged a salute with the original *Queen Mary* which is berthed at the port. On her first world cruise *Queen Mary 2* met *Queen Elizabeth 2* at Sydney on the 20 February 2007. It was the first time that two Cunard Queens had been together in Sydney since the original *Queen Mary* and *Queen Elizabeth* had been there on trooping duties in 1941.

The keel of *Queen Victoria* was laid on the 12 May 2006 and the superstructure floated out in January the following year. She commenced her trails on the 24 August 2007 and was named by Her Royal Highness the Duchess of Cornwall at Southampton and sailed on her maiden cruise on the 11 December that year. At 92,000 tons she is the second largest Cunard vessel ever owned by the line. At the start of her first world cruise she sailed in tandem across the Atlantic with *Queen Elizabeth 2* meeting *Queen Mary 2* in New York on the 13 January 2008.

Cunard announced the sale of *Queen Elizabeth 2* and following her final voyage she was handed over to Nakheel at Dubai on the 27 November 2008 to be used as a hotel, restaurant and entertainment complex. An order was placed with Fincantieri's Monfalcone Shipyard at Trieste in Italy and on the 10 October 2007 Cunard announced that she would be namd *Queen Elizabeth*. *Queen Elizabeth* sailed on her maiden voyage in October 2010 from Southampton and incorporates 1046 cabins on board, eighty five per cent of these are outside and 71 per cent have balconies. There is also the Verandah Grills, a Grand Lobby, Midships Bar, Yacht Club, Queens Room, Lido Restaurant, Library, Commodore Club, Royal Court Theatre, Britannia Restaurant and games deck.

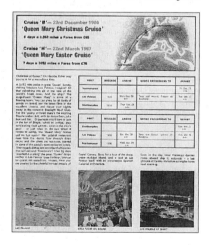

Brochure detailing the *Queen Mary* 1966 Christmas Cruise and 1967 Easter Cruise from Southampton to Las Palmas.

Britannic was built in 1930 for the White Star Line, which amalgamated with Cunard in 1934 to form the Cunard-White Star Line. She was converted to troop transport in 1939 and resumed commercial service in May 1948. In June 1950 Britannic collided with an American cargo vessel in New York Harbour. She was laid up with a broken crankshaft in 1960 and arrived at the shipbreakers at Inverkeithing in December that year.

Remuera was built in 1948 as the Cunard passenger-cargo liner *Parthia*. She was 13,362grt and 162m by 21m with a service speed of 17 knots. She was sold to the New Zealand Shipping Company in 1961 and is shown here preparing to sail on her maiden voyage for the company from Liverpool Landing Stage in May 1962. She was transferred to the Eastern & Australian Steam Ship Company in 1965 and renamed *Aramac* for their Melbourne to Hong Kong and Japan route. She was broken up at Kaohsiung in 1969.

Mauretania was built by Cammell Laird at Birkenhead in 1939. She was the largest liner to be built in England at the time and was converted to a troopship in 1940 at Sydney, Australia. She was returned to the Cunard Line in 1946 and overhauled by Cammell Laird, resuming transatlantic service when she sailed from Liverpool to New York on 26 April 1947. In 1962 she was painted in 'Caronia' green and is shown in Gladstone Graving Dock in Liverpool in November 1963. Following an unsuccessful period on the New York to Cannes, Genoa and Naples service, she was sold to the shipbreakers at Inverkeithing in 1965.

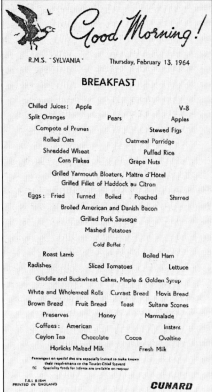

Good Morning!

R.M.S. "SYLVANIA" Thursday, February 13, 1964

BREAKFAST

Chilled Juices: Apple V-8

Split Oranges Pears Apples

Compote of Prunes Stewed Figs

Rolled Oats Oatmeal Porridge

Shredded Wheat Puffed Rice

Corn Flakes Grape Nuts

Grilled Yarmouth Bloaters, Maître d'Hôtel
Grilled Fillet of Haddock au Citron

Eggs: Fried Turned Boiled Poached Shirred

Broiled American and Danish Bacon

Grilled Pork Sausage

Mashed Potatoes

Cold Buffet :

Roast Lamb Boiled Ham

Radishes Sliced Tomatoes Lettuce

Griddle and Buckwheat Cakes, Maple & Golden Syrup

White and Wholemeal Rolls Currant Bread Hovis Bread

Brown Bread Fruit Bread Toast Sultana Scones

Preserves Honey Marmalade

Coffees: American Instant

Ceylon Tea Chocolate Cocoa Ovaltine

Horlicks Malted Milk Fresh Milk

Passengers on special diet are especially invited to make known
their requirements on the Tourist Chief Steward
fC Speciality foods for infants are available on request

T.S.I. B 1844
PRINTED IN ENGLAND **CUNARD**

Menu for breakfast on *Sylvania* (1957/21,989grt) for Thursday, 13 February 1964.

Opposite page: Caronia was one of the most successful liners owned by the Cunard Line. She was built by John Brown & Co. on the Clyde, launched on 30 October 1947 and was employed on the transatlantic service as well as completing a regular World Cruise schedule. This photograph was taken in Southampton in May 1966. In the following year she was laid up in that port and in May 1968 she was sold to Universal Line SA and renamed *Columbia* and then *Caribia*. She was sold again to the Franchard Corporation and, while on a cruise in 1969, suffered an engine room explosion off St Thomas. She was towed to New York and laid up there until she was sold to the shipbreakers in Kaohsiung in 1974. However, on the tow to Taiwan she drifted ashore at Guam and broke into three pieces. She was later demolished.

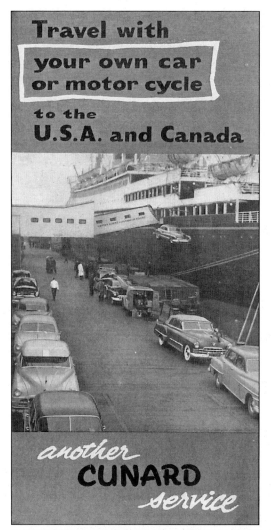

Travel with your own car or motor cycle to the U.S.A. and Canada

another **CUNARD** *service*

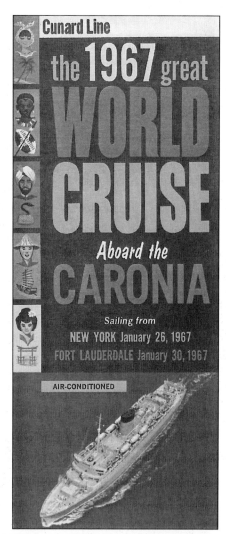

Cunard Line

the **1967** great **WORLD CRUISE**

Aboard the **CARONIA**

Sailing from
NEW YORK January 26, 1967
FORT LAUDERDALE January 30, 1967

AIR-CONDITIONED

CRUISES FROM AMERICA

1960

"CARONIA" WEST INDIES CRUISES

14 DAYS   **FROM £129**

PORTS OF CALL	ARRIVE	LEAVE
	1960	1960
NEW YORK		Wed., Aug. 31 a.m.
PORT-AU-PRINCE	Sat., Sept. 3 a.m.	Sat., Sept. 3 Midn't
ST. THOMAS	Mon., Sept. 5 a.m.	Mon., Sept. 5 a.m.
MARTINIQUE	Tues., Sept. 6 a.m.	Tues., Sept. 6 p.m.
TRINIDAD	Wed., Sept. 7 a.m.	Wed., Sept. 7 p.m.
LA GUAIRA	Thur., Sept. 8 a.m.	Thur., Sept. 8 p.m.
CURACAO	Fri., Sept. 9 a.m.	Sat., Sept. 10 a.m.
NASSAU	Mon., Sept. 12 a.m.	Mon., Sept. 12 p.m.
NEW YORK	Wed., Sept. 14 a.m.	

12 DAYS   **FROM £113**

PORTS OF CALL	ARRIVE	LEAVE
	1960	1960
NEW YORK		Sat., Sept. 17 a.m.
ST. THOMAS	Tues., Sept. 20 p.m.	Wed., Sept. 21 a.m.
LA GUAIRA	Thur., Sept. 22 a.m.	Thur., Sept. 22 p.m.
CURACAO	Fri., Sept. 23 a.m.	Fri., Sept. 23 p.m.
PORT-AU-PRINCE	Sun., Sept. 25 a.m.	Mon., Sept. 26 a.m.
NASSAU	Tues., Sept. 27 a.m.	Tues., Sept. 27 p.m.
NEW YORK	Thur., Sept. 29 p.m.	

"CARONIA" AUTUMN MEDITERRANEAN & BLACK SEA CRUISE

58 DAYS   **FROM £393**

PORTS OF CALL	ARRIVE	LEAVE
	1960	1960
NEW YORK		Tues., Oct. 4 a.m.
MADEIRA	Mon., Oct. 10 a.m.	Mon., Oct. 10 a.m.
CASABLANCA	Wed., Oct. 12 a.m.	Fri., Oct. 14 a.m.
TANGIER	Fri., Oct. 14 Noon	Sat., Oct. 15 a.m.
MALTA	Mon., Oct. 17 a.m.	Mon., Oct. 17 p.m.
DARDANELLES	Wed., Oct. 19 a.m.	Cruising
YALTA	Thur., Oct. 20 a.m.	Thur., Oct. 20 p.m.
ODESSA	Fri., Oct. 21 a.m.	Fri., Oct. 21 p.m.
CONSTANTA	Sat., Oct. 22 a.m.	Sat., Oct. 22 p.m.
ISTANBUL	Sun., Oct. 23 p.m.	Mon., Oct. 24 a.m.
ALEXANDRIA	Wed., Oct. 26 a.m.	Sun., Oct. 30 p.m.
HAIFA	Mon., Oct. 31 a.m.	Tues., Nov. 1 p.m.
ATHENS	Thur., Nov. 3 a.m.	Thur., Nov. 3 p.m.
DUBROVNIK	Sat., Nov. 5 a.m.	Sat., Nov. 5 p.m.
VENICE	Sun., Nov. 6 a.m.	Tues., Nov. 8 p.m.
CATANIA	Thur., Nov. 10 a.m.	Thur., Nov. 10 Noon
MESSINA	Thur., Nov. 10 p.m.	Thur., Nov. 10 p.m.
NAPLES	Fri., Nov. 11 a.m.	Sun., Nov. 13 p.m.
VILLEFRANCHE	Mon., Nov. 14 a.m.	Tues., Nov. 15 p.m.
BARCELONA	Wed., Nov. 16 a.m.	Thur., Nov. 17 a.m.
PALMA	Thur., Nov. 17 a.m.	Thur., Nov. 17 Midn't
MALAGA	Sat., Nov. 19 a.m.	Sun., Nov. 20 a.m.
GIBRALTAR	Sun., Nov. 20 a.m.	Sun., Nov. 20 p.m.
LISBON	Mon., Nov. 21 a.m.	Tues., Nov. 22 p.m.
CHERBOURG	Thur., Nov. 24 a.m.	Thur., Nov. 24 p.m.
SOUTHAMPTON	Fri., Nov. 25 a.m.	

1961

"BRITANNIC" MEDITERRANEAN CRUISE

66 DAYS   **FROM £455**

PORTS OF CALL	ARRIVE	LEAVE
	1961	1961
NEW YORK		Fri., Jan. 20 p.m.
MADEIRA	Sat., Jan. 28 a.m.	Sat., Jan. 28 p.m.
CASABLANCA	Mon., Jan. 30 a.m.	Tues., Jan. 31 Midn't
TANGIER	Wed., Feb. 1 p.m.	Thur., Feb. 2 a.m.
ALGIERS	Fri., Feb. 3 a.m.	Fri., Feb. 3 p.m.
MALTA	Sun., Feb. 5 a.m.	Sun., Feb. 5 p.m.
ALEXANDRIA	Wed., Feb. 8 a.m.	Sun., Feb. 12 p.m.
HAIFA	Mon., Feb. 13 a.m.	Wed., Feb. 15 p.m.
LARNACA	Thur., Feb. 16 a.m.	Thur., Feb. 16 p.m.
RHODES	Fri., Feb. 17 Noon	Fri., Feb. 17 p.m.
ISTANBUL	Sun., Feb. 19 a.m.	Cruising
ISTANBUL	Sun., Feb. 19 p.m.	Tues., Feb. 21 a.m.
DARDANELLES	Tues., Feb. 21 p.m.	Cruising
ATHENS	Wed., Feb. 22 p.m.	Thur., Feb. 23 p.m.
DUBROVNIK	Sat., Feb. 25 a.m.	Sat., Feb. 25 p.m.
VENICE	Sun., Feb. 26 p.m.	Tues., Feb. 28 p.m.
MESSINA	Thur., Mar. 2 a.m.	Thur., Mar. 2 p.m.
NAPLES	Fri., Mar. 3 a.m.	Mon., Mar. 6 a.m.
VILLEFRANCHE	Tues., Mar. 7 a.m.	Thur., Mar. 9 p.m.
BARCELONA	Fri., Mar. 10 a.m.	Fri., Mar. 10 Midn't
PALMA	Sat., Mar. 11 a.m.	Sat., Mar. 11 Midn't
MALAGA	Mon., Mar. 13 a.m.	Tues., Mar. 14 Midn't
GIBRALTAR	Wed., Mar. 15 a.m.	Wed., Mar. 15 p.m.
LISBON	Thur., Mar. 16 a.m.	Sat., Mar. 18 p.m.
CHERBOURG	Mon., Mar. 20 a.m.	Mon., Mar. 20 a.m.
SOUTHAMPTON	Mon., Mar. 20 p.m.	

"CARONIA" WORLD CRUISE

95 DAYS   **FROM £1027**

PORTS OF CALL	ARRIVE	LEAVE
	1961	1961
NEW YORK		Sat., Jan. 28 p.m.
TRINIDAD	Thur., Feb. 2 a.m.	Thur., Feb. 2 p.m.
RIO DE JANEIRO	Tues., Feb. 9 p.m.	Sat., Feb. 11 a.m.
CAPE TOWN	Sat., Feb. 18 a.m.	Mon., Feb. 20 p.m.
DURBAN	Wed., Feb. 22 p.m.	Sat., Feb. 25 p.m.
ZANZIBAR	Wed., Mar. 1 a.m.	Wed., Mar. 1 p.m.
MOMBASA	Thur., Mar. 2 a.m.	Thur., Mar. 2 p.m.
PORT VICTORIA	Sun., Mar. 5 a.m.	Sun., Mar. 5 p.m.
BOMBAY	Thur., Mar. 9 a.m.	Wed., Mar. 15 a.m.
COLOMBO	Fri., Mar. 17 a.m.	Sat., Mar. 18 p.m.
SINGAPORE	Wed., Mar. 22 a.m.	Thur., Mar. 23 a.m.
BANGKOK	Sat., Mar. 25 a.m.	Sun., Mar. 26 a.m.
HONG KONG	Wed., Mar. 29 a.m.	Fri., Mar. 31 a.m.
KOBE	Mon., Apr. 3 a.m.	Wed., Apr. 5 Noon
YOKOHAMA	Thur., Apr. 6 a.m.	Sat., Apr. 8 p.m.
HONOLULU	Sat., Apr. 15 a.m.	Sun., Apr. 16 p.m.
LONG BEACH	Fri., Apr. 21 a.m.	Sat., Apr. 22 a.m.
ACAPULCO	Tues., Apr. 25 a.m.	Tues., Apr. 25 p.m.
BALBOA	Fri., Apr. 28 p.m.	Sat., Apr. 29 p.m.
CRISTOBAL	Sat., Apr. 29 p.m.	Sat., Apr. 29 p.m.
NEW YORK	Wed., May 3 p.m.	

"CARONIA" SPRING CRUISE

39 DAYS   **FROM £348**

PORTS OF CALL	ARRIVE	LEAVE
	1961	1961
NEW YORK		Mon., May 8 p.m.
MADEIRA	Sun., May 14 p.m.	Sun., May 14 p.m.
TANGIER	Tues., May 16 a.m.	Tues., May 16 p.m.
PALMA	Wed., May 17 p.m.	Wed., May 17 p.m.
MALTA	Fri., May 19 a.m.	Fri., May 19 p.m.
ATHENS	Sat., May 20 p.m.	Sun., May 21 Midn't
DUBROVNIK	Tues., May 23 p.m.	Tues., May 23 p.m.
VENICE	Wed., May 24 a.m.	Thur., May 25 p.m.
CATANIA	Sat., May 27 a.m.	Sat., May 27 Noon
MESSINA	Sat., May 27 p.m.	Sat., May 27 p.m.
NAPLES	Sun., May 28 a.m.	Tues., May 30 p.m.
VILLEFRANCHE	Wed., May 31 p.m.	Thur., June 1 p.m.
BARCELONA	Fri., June 2 a.m.	Sat., June 3 a.m.
MALAGA	Sun., June 4 a.m.	Sun., June 4 Midn't
GIBRALTAR	Mon., June 5 a.m.	Mon., June 5 p.m.
LISBON	Tues., June 6 a.m.	Wed., June 7 p.m.
CHERBOURG	Fri., June 9 a.m.	Fri., June 9 a.m.
SOUTHAMPTON	Fri., June 9 p.m.	

Details of 1960 *Caronia* cruises and a sixty-six day Britannic Mediterranean cruise from New York in 1961.

CUNARD QUALITY CRUISES

**ATLANTIC ISLES
WEST INDIES
MEDITERRANEAN**

**BIG SHIP CRUISING
AT ITS BEST**

QUEEN MARY
MAURETANIA

		Sails	Days	Miles	From
A	**"QUEEN MARY" CHRISTMAS CRUISE.** To Las Palmas.	Dec 23rd 1964	6	3,052	£65
B	**"QUEEN MARY" NEW YEAR CRUISE.** To Las Palmas.	Dec 30th 1964	6	3,052	£65
C	**"QUEEN MARY" FEBRUARY SUNSHINE CRUISE.** Calling at Gibraltar and Las Palmas.	Feb 15th 1965	8	3,369	£85
1	**"MAURETANIA" ATLANTIC ISLES AND WEST AFRICA CHRISTMAS CRUISE.** Calling at Ponta Delgada, Madeira, St. Vincent, Dakar, Las Palmas, Casablanca, Tangier and Gibraltar.	Dec 23rd 1964	20	6,116	£140
2	**"MAURETANIA" WEST INDIES CRUISE.** Calling at Las Palmas, Nassau, Port Everglades, Kingston, Colon, Curacao, La Guaira, Trinidad, Grenada, Barbados, Martinique, St. Thomas and Madeira.	Jan 15th 1965	37	12,213	£280
3	**"MAURETANIA" ATLANTIC ISLES CRUISE.** Calling at Madeira, Tenerife, Las Palmas, Casablanca, Gibraltar and Lisbon.	Feb 24th 1965	13	3,548	£85
4	**"MAURETANIA" MEDITERRANEAN CRUISE.** Calling at Tangier, Barcelona, Livorno, Catania and Palma.	Mar 10th 1965	14	4,744	£93
5	**"MAURETANIA" MEDITERRANEAN CRUISE.** Calling at Tangier, Villefranche, Naples and Palma.	Mar 25th 1965	13	4,456	£85
6	**"MAURETANIA" EASTER MEDITERRANEAN CRUISE.** Calling at Tangier, Naples, Beirut, Haifa, Malta and Gibraltar.	Apr 10th 1965	20	6,539	£140
7	**"MAURETANIA" MEDITERRANEAN CRUISE.** Calling at Gibraltar, Villefranche, Barcelona, Palma, Malaga and Tangier.	May 1st 1965	13	3,901	£85
8	**"MAURETANIA" MEDITERRANEAN CRUISE.** Calling at Tangier, Naples, Palma and Gibraltar.	May 15th 1965	13	4,385	£85

Details of 'Cunard Quality Cruises' to the Atlantic Isles, West Indies and Mediterranean by *Queen Mary* and *Mauretania* from Southampton in Winter 1964/65.

Carinthia was launched by Princess Margaret at John Brown's Yard on 14 December 1955 for the Liverpool-Canada service. She took the last Cunard passenger sailing from Liverpool to Montreal on 13 October 1967 and returned to Southampton where she was laid up. She was sold to the Sitmar Line in 1968, and renamed *Fairland*. Converted to a cruise liner at Trieste in 1970, she was renamed *Fairsea* in 1971. In 1988 Sitmar Cruises were sold to the P&O Line and she was renamed *Fair Princess*, becoming *China Seas Discovery* in 2000 when she was acquired by Emerald Cruises.

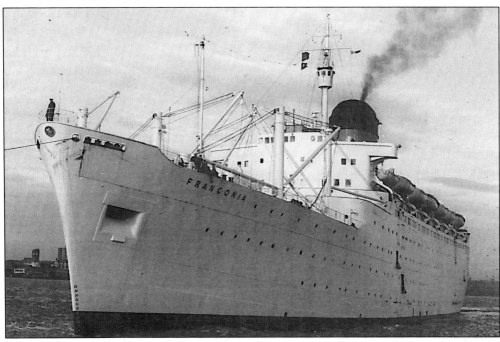

Franconia was built as *Saxonia* for Cunard's Liverpool-Canada service. She was renamed *Franconia* in 1963 and painted with a green hull for cruising out of New York and Port Everglades. She was employed on Bermuda sailings in 1968 and given a white hull. In 1972 she was laid up in the River Fal with her sister *Carmania* and was sold the following year, becoming the Russian liner *Fedor Shalyapin*.

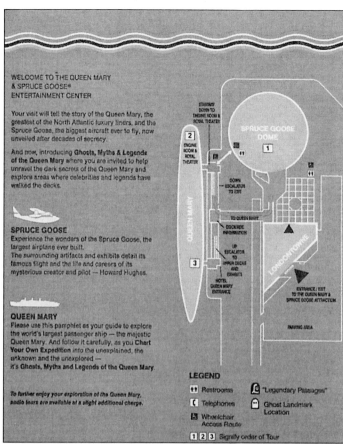

WELCOME TO THE QUEEN MARY & SPRUCE GOOSE® ENTERTAINMENT CENTER

Your visit will tell the story of the Queen Mary, the greatest of the North Atlantic luxury liners, and the Spruce Goose, the biggest aircraft ever to fly, now unveiled after decades of secrecy.

And now, introducing Ghosts, Myths & Legends of the Queen Mary where you are invited to help unravel the dark secrets of the Queen Mary and explore areas where celebrities and legends have walked the decks.

SPRUCE GOOSE

Experience the wonders of the Spruce Goose, the largest airplane ever built.
The surrounding artifacts and exhibits detail its famous flight and the life and careers of its mysterious creator and pilot — Howard Hughes.

QUEEN MARY

Please use this pamphlet as your guide to explore the world's largest passenger ship — the majestic Queen Mary. And follow it carefully, as you **Chart Your Own Expedition** into the unexplained, the unknown and the unexplored —
it's Ghosts, Myths and Legends of the Queen Mary.

To further enjoy your exploration of the Queen Mary, audio tours are available at a slight additional charge.

LEGEND

†† Restrooms   🎧 "Legendary Passages"

☎ Telephones   Ghost Landmark Location

♿ Wheelchair Access Route

1 2 3 Signify order of Tour

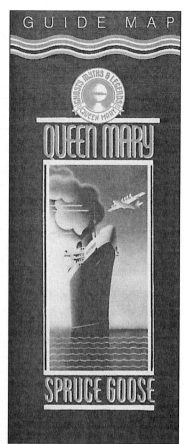

Queen Mary at Long Beach, California.

Sylvania (1957/21,989grt) was the last of the four Saxonia class vessels to enter service and replaced the *Britannic* on the Liverpool-New York route in 1961. In 1965 she made the first cruise out of Liverpool since 1939 and the final Cunard Liverpool-New York sailing in 1966. She was painted with a white hull in 1967 and, after making the final Cunard New York-Liverpool sailing, she was laid up at Southampton. In 1968 she was sold to Sitmar Line and was renamed *Fairwind* but remained at Southampton until 1970 when she was converted at Trieste. She was renamed *Sitmar Fairwind* in 1988 and *Dawn Princess* when the line was aquired by P&O in 1988. In 1993 she was bought by Happy Days Shipping and renamed *Albatros*.

Cunard Countess (1975/17,495grt) was built by Burmeister & Wain Skibs., at Copenhagen and fitted out by Industrie Navali Merchaniche Affini at La Spezia. She replaced the *Cunard Adventurer* and sailed on cruises from San Juan to La Guaira, Grenada, Barbados, St. Lucia and St Thomas. In 1982 she carried troops from the Ascension Islands to the Falklands. In 1996 she was purchased by Awani Modern Hotels, Indonesia and became the *Awani Dream 2* and *Olympic Countess* in 1998 when she was bought by Epirotiki and Sun Lines.

Cunard Princess (1977/17,496grt) was launched as the *Cunard Conquest* but was renamed *Cunard Princess* by Princess Grace of Monoco at New York on 1 January 1977. She operated from Bermuda, Florida and also completed Panama Canal voyages. She was purchased by Mediterranean Shipping Cruises, Geneva in 1995 and renamed *Rhapsody*.

Cunard Freight Services

The Cunard Cargo Liners "Andria" and "Alsatia", 7,226 tons gross. 10,750 tons deadweight.

LIVERPOOL TO NEW YORK

		Receiving Cargo
MEDIA		Jan. 25th to Feb. 1st
SYLVANIA	(via Greenock & Halifax, N.S.)	Feb. 2nd to Feb. 7th
ARABIA		Feb. 8th to Feb. 15th
CARINTHIA	(via Greenock & Halifax, N.S.)	Feb. 16th to Feb. 21st
PARTHIA		Feb. 22nd to Mar. 1st
SYLVANIA	(via Greenock & Halifax, N.S.)	Mar. 2nd to Mar. 7th

LIVERPOOL TO HALIFAX N.S.

*SYLVANIA	(via Greenock)	Feb. 2nd to Feb. 7th
COLINA		Feb. 2nd to Feb. 8th
*CARINTHIA	(via Greenock)	Feb. 16th to Feb. 21st
SANTONA		Feb. 22nd to Mar. 1st

*Cargo by special arrangement only.

LIVERPOOL TO ST. JOHN N.B.

COLINA	(via Halifax, N.S.)	Feb. 2nd to Feb. 8th
SANTONA	(via Halifax, N.S.)	Feb. 22nd to Mar. 1st

LIVERPOOL TO HOUSTON, NEW ORLEANS, GALVESTON, MOBILE & TAMPA

IRISH LARCH	(via Glasgow)	Feb. 20th to Feb. 25th (noon

LOADING BERTH : HUSKISSON DOCK

Bills of Lading must be presented by Shippers or Agents not later than the day after vessel's closing date.

THE CUNARD STEAM-SHIP COMPANY LIMITED,

Telegrams : "CUNARD."
Telegrams : "CUNARDSTAR." **CUNARD BUILDING, LIVERPOOL, 3.** Telephone : CENtral 9201

LONDON, E.C.3.	...88, LEADENHALL STREET	BRADFORD	... LEEDS ROAD
BIRMINGHAM, 2	...8, TEMPLE STREET	BRISTOL, I	II, PARK STREET
MANCHESTER, 2	...74, CROSS STREET	SOUTHAMPTON	CANUTE ROAD

BIRMINGHAM	J. JOHNSON & CO. LTD., 32, PARADISE STREET
HULL	G. A. WOODCOCK, LTD., THE AVENUE, HIGH STREET
NEWCASTLE-ON-TYNE	WM. MILBURN & CO., LTD., MILBURN HOUSE
SHEFFIELD, 3.	G. A. WOODCOCK, LTD., 27, THE WICKER
NORTHAMPTON	MORISON, POLLEXFEN & BLAIR, LTD., BEACON BUILDINGS, WOOD STREET
STOKE-ON-TRENT	MORISON, POLLEXFEN & BLAIR, LTD., FEDERATION HOUSE, STATION ROAD
GLASGOW, C.2	THOMAS MEADOWS & CO., LTD., 127, ST. VINCENT STREET
DUNDEE	THOS. & JNO. BROCKLEBANK, LTD., 8, PANMURE STREET
LEITH, EDINBURGH, 5	CURRIE LINE LTD., TRINITY COTTAGE, GOLDENACRE
BELFAST, I	LITTLE, WHITING & TEDFORD, LTD. 74, HIGH STREET

| 1/69 No. 23 | **SUBJECT TO CHANGE WITHOUT NOTICE** | 1/2/61 |
| B. 1446 | | P.T.O. PRINTED IN ENGLAND |

Cunard Freight Services notice for the Liverpool to New York, Halifax, St John's, Houston, New Orleans, Galveston, Mobile and Tampa services for January, February and March 1961.

Scythia (1964/5,837grt) was built by Cammell Laird & Company for North West Line (Mersey) Ltd on long-term bareboat charter to Cunard. She was purchased by Cunard in 1969 and was sold to T&J Harrison who renamed her *Merchant*. She became *Sisal Trader* in 1979 and sank in cyclone Kamisy off Mayotte Island, Madagascar in 1984. She was refloated on 16 April 1984 and towed to Gadani Beach where she was broken up in 1986.

Alaunia, 1960, Cunard Steamship Company, 7,004grt, 149m by 19m, 17½ knots. She was transferred to the Brocklebank Line in 1969, becoming the *Malancha*. She was then sold by the group in 1971 and renamed *Humi Nastta*, *Yungming* in 1973 and *Hong Qi No. 108* in 1975. She was broken up in 1993.

Ben My Chree (1966/2,762grt), *Servia* (1971/8,557grt), *Samaria* (1973/8,557grt), *Saxonia* (1971/8,547grt), *England* (1964/8,221grt) and *Scythia* (1972/8,557grt) laid up in Vittoria Dock, Birkenhead in 1985.

Port Albany, 1965, Port Line, 8,362grt, 149m by 21m, 18 knots. She became *Marietta* in 1972, *Artemon* in 1991 and arrived at Alang for breaking up on 15 May 1992.

Port Wyndham, 1935, Port Line, 8,580grt, 151m by 20m, 14 knots. On 11 April 1945 she was torpedoed by a German submarine off Lade Buoy, Dungeness, and was towed to Southampton and later the Clyde for repairs. She arrived at Osaka on 23 January 1967 for breaking up.

BROCKLEBANK LINE
TO
CALCUTTA
AND CHALNA
ALSO TAKING CARGO FOR PORT SAID, SUEZ AND ADEN

VESSEL	CLOSING DATES	
	GLASGOW	BIRKENHEAD
*MASKELIYA	—	16th MAY
†MAIHAR	20th MAY	29th MAY
*MARKHOR (Closing NEWPORT 30th MAY)	—	10th JUNE
MANDASOR	—	23rd JUNE

† NOT TAKING CARGO FOR PORT SAID ★ REFRIGERATOR SPACE AVAILABLE

Sth. Wales berth also covered in June with liberty to coast to Birkenhead at shippers risk

Loading Berths : Glasgow : 20/21 Princes Dock
Birkenhead : Vittoria Wharf, East Float

Cargo should be despatched only on receipt of a calling forward notice and to avoid congestion shippers are requested to deliver on the date specified.
Goods intended for shipment by the vessel named in this Notice will be subject to the terms and conditions of the Brocklebank Line Shipping Note and Bill of Lading.
All cargo should be distinctly marked with the name of the port of destination.

For Rates of Freight and further particulars apply to the Agents overleaf or to the Owners:

THOS. & JNO. BROCKLEBANK LTD.

Telephone CENtral 6633. CUNARD BUILDING, LIVERPOOL 3

BRANCH OFFICES :

57 Princess Street	1 Vicar Lane	34 Wellington St.	95 Colmore Row	8 Panmure Street
MANCHESTER 2	SHEFFIELD 1	LEEDS 1	BIRMINGHAM 3	DUNDEE
Tel. CENtral 3709/3700	Tel. 28925/6	Tel. 32885	Tel. CENtral 6745	Tel. 3005/6

11/5/59

Brockebank Line sailing notice dated 11 May 1959.

Mathura, 1969, Brocklebank Line, 8,782grt, 151m by 19m, 17 knots. She was sold in 1972 and renamed *Euryton*, and *Alwaha* in 1976. She suffered an engine room fire in September 1977 at Aden and was broken up at Gadani Beach in 1978.

Malakand, 1942, Brocklebank Line, 8,078grt, 151m by 19m, 13½knots. She arrived at Kaohsiung on 13 December 1966 for breaking up.

BROCKLEBANK LINE

POSITION OF STEAMERS

X 39   MAGDAPUR   Left   Mukalla 19th January (Gan, Madras & Calcutta).

X 43   MAHANADA   Arrd. Lay-by berth Colombo 11th January (To be arranged).

X 2   MAHOUT   Left   Milford Haven 17th January (Suez, Aden & Calcutta).

X 34   MAHRONDA   Arrd. Graythorpe 8th December (Lloyds Special Survey).

X 32   MAHSEER   Berthed Colombo 14th January (To be arranged).

X 36   MAIDAN   Left   Rotterdam 11th January (Port Said, Suez, Jeddah, Massawa, Djibouti, Aden, Assab & Colombo VIA Ceuta).

X 25   MAIPURA   Arrd. off Colombo 15th January (To be arranged).

X 16   MAKRANA   Arrd. Middlesbrough 15th January (Port Said, Suez, Aqaba, Assab, Djibouti, Berbera, Aden, Mukalla, Gan, Male, Madras & Calcutta VIA Bremen, Hamburg & London).

   42   MALAKAND   Arrd. Manchester 13th January (Cardiff & Liverpool).

X 34   MANAAR   Left   Middlesbrough 19th January (Port Said, Suez, Massawa, Djibouti, Aden, Assab & Colombo VIA Antwerp, Bremen, London & Rotterdam).

   12   MANGLA   Arrd. Savannah 17th January (Gulfport, New Orleans, Mobile, Corpus Christi, Galveston & Houston).

   36   MANIPUR   Left   Trincomalee 18th January (London, Manchester, Liverpool & Dublin VIA Djibouti, Massawa & Port Sudan

    2   MARKHOR   Arrd. Liverpool 18th January (Manchester & London).

X 55   MARTAND   Arrd. London 15th January (Suez, Aqaba, Jeddah, Berbera, Aden, Mukalla, Seychelles, Gan, Trincomalee, Madras, Calcutta & Chittagong).

   15   MASIRAH   Left   Calcutta 15th January (Wilmington Del., Savannah, New Orleans, Galveston, & Houston VIA Djibouti).

   22   MASKELIYA   Arrd. Dunkirk 18th January (Bremen & Dundee).

X 9   MATHURA   Arrd. Chittagong 18th January (Loads for U.S.A. Gulf Ports VIA Chalna, Calcutta, Colombo & Djibouti).

   36   MATRA   Left   Colombo 18th January (Liverpool, London, Boulogne, Dunkirk, Antwerp, Bremen & Dundee VIA Djibouti).

X 20   MATURATA   Arrd. Glasgow 15th January (Loads Glasgow & Birkenhead for Malta, Port Said, Suez, Aden & Calcutta).

   12   MAWANA   Left   Visakhapatnam 16th January (London, Boulogne, Liverpool & Dundee VIA Colombo).

X 3   PORT CHALMERS Arrd. off Colombo 26th December (For redelivery to Owners)

X 1   RIVERTON Berthed Calcutta 7th January (London & Manchester VIA Trincomalee & Djibouti).

    1   INCHDOUGLAS   Left Port Said 15th January (London, Manchester & Dublin VIA Djibouti).

Brocklebank Line position of steamers list dated 20 January 1964.

Masirah, 1957, Brocklebank Line, 8,733grt, 151m by 19m, 15½knots. She was sold in 1972 and renamed *Eurysthenes*. She grounded off the Philippines in May 1974 and, as it was uneconomical to repair her, she was broken up at Kaohsiung later that year.

Mangla, 1959, Brocklebank Line, 8,805grt, 151m by 19m, 16½knots. She was renamed *Euryplus* in 1972. In November 1975 she was damaged by a serious fire, following an explosion in her engine room. The damage was so extensive that she was sold to shipbreakers. She left Los Angeles in tow on 1 March 1976 and arrived at Kaohsiung on 4 April.

Two

Ocean Group

S.S. "TYNDAREUS"
KAPAL HAJI SEROMBONG BIRU

Tyndareus, 1916, Blue Funnel Line, 11,347grt, 155m by 19m, $13\frac{1}{2}$knots. She was broken up at Hong Kong in 1961.

In 1852 Alfred Holt purchased the *Dumbarton Youth* a three-masted sailing ship which was fitted with two direct action engines and, as he was a railway engineer, he was able to replace the engines with those of his own design. He had trained as a railway engineer but because of a recession in the railway business he took a job as a clerk with his brother's shipping firm, Lamport & Holt Line. He soon began to look at the prospects of operating a service to the Far East, and was joined by his brother Phillip.

The early sailings were restricted to the coasting trade and to French ports but in 1855 sailings to the West Indies were advertised. In 1865 the brothers formed the Ocean Steamship Co. and ordered three steamships from Scotts of Greenock which were designed as square-rigged barques of 2,300 gross tons with tandem compound engines.

On 19 April 1866 the first of these, *Agamemnon*, sailed from Liverpool to the Far East, calling at Penang, Singapore, Hong Kong and Shanghai. She was followed by the *Ajax* on 30 June and the *Achilles* on 30 September that year. These vessels proved to be very economical to operate and *Achilles* took fifty-seven days and eighteen hours to return home from China via the Cape. She carried 2,800 tons of cargo and on her voyage of 12,352 miles consumed less than 20 tons of coal a day.

In March 1870 *Diomed* became the company's first ship to use the Suez Canal which had been opened the previous year. Sailings from London were operated briefly in 1880 and by 1883 it became a port of discharge only when a regular weekly service operated from the Port of Liverpool to China and later Japan.

Captain Frank Pitts was sent to Australia by Alfred Holt in 1889 to 'look at the prospects and report on the possibilities of running a service from Fremantle up the coast of Western Australia via Java to Singapore'. The *Saladin* and *Sultan* were built in 1890 for this service and an agreement was made with the West Australian Steam Ship Co. to run a joint fortnightly service on this route.

To avoid cabotage problems a Dutch subsidiary, NSM 'Oceaan', was formed in 1891 to operate a regular service from the United Kingdom and Holland to Java and Sumatra. The outward cargoes comprised manufactured goods with raw material, rubber, tobacco, rice and tea on the homeward journey. These vessels flew the Dutch ensign.

Antenor, 1925, Blue Funnel Line, 11,345grt. She was broken up at Blyth in 1953.

Charon, 1936, Blue Funnel Line, 3,703grt, 102m by 16m, 14 knots. She was sold in 1964 and renamed *Seng Hong No.1*, and broken up at Singapore in 1965.

A cargo service to Australia was started in 1901 with vessels loading at Glasgow and later at Liverpool. In 1910 *Aeneas, Ascanius* and *Anchises* enabled the company to provide a passenger service on this route calling at South Africa on the way to Australia. *Nestor* and *Ulysses* followed in 1913 carrying apples, timber and sugar and refrigerated cargos such as meat and butter on the inward voyages. *Nestor* made her last voyage in 1950 after giving the company thirty-eight years service in peace and two world wars.

The Ocean Steam Ship Co. became a Limited Company in 1902 when the China Mutual Steam Navigation Co. was taken over. It had been in operation since 1882 and traded from China to parts of Canada and the United States. The line started sailings between the Straits Settlements, Java and the Pacific coast of America and later from China, Japan and the West Coast of America. The opening of the Panama Canal in 1914 enabled the company to provide a service from the United Kingdom to the West Coast of America.

In the First World War, the Blue Funnel Line lost sixteen ships and had twenty-nine others damaged by shellfire, torpedos or mines. The Indra Line was purchased in 1915 enabling the Line to provide a regular service between New York and the Far East. In 1917 the Knight Line was aquired with the four ships of their fleet. At the end of the War several ships were fitted with temporary passenger accommodation at the request of the British Government. The steam turbine vessels *Sarpedon, Patroclus, Hector* and *Antenor* were introduced from 1923 and were the company's first ships with substantial passenger accommodation.

From 1919 to 1934 the company ordered forty-eight new vessels and in 1935 they acquired the London-based Glen Line which retained its own red funnel and traditional Glen names. In 1936 the Ocean Steam Ship Co. purchased 675,000 shares in Elder Dempster Lines Holdings Ltd, becoming the largest shareholder and taking control of the company. The origins of the Line can be traced back to the 1830s but it was not until 1868 that Elder, Dempster & Co. was appointed as the agency to run a shipping service from Glasgow and Liverpool to West Africa. Alfred Jones was given a junior partnership in Elder Dempster Line in 1879, when the line operated twenty-one ships, and by 1884 he controlled the company. On his death the line was acquired by Sir Owen Cosby Phillips and Lord Pirrie forming Elder Dempster & Co. Ltd.

In the Second World War, the Blue Funnel Line lost forty-four ships with a gross tonnage of 349,320 which was more than half of their fleet. The completion of the War saw the purchase of several 'Victory' and 'Liberty' ships to enable services to be provided while new ships were being built in various British shipyards.

Initially, three classes of vessels were introduced which were the *Anchises*, *Peleus* and *Helenus* types. The first A-class vessel was *Calchas*, which was built by Harland & Wolff in 1947. The company instituted their own training scheme for midshipmen, engineers and stewards and the *Calchas* was used as their training ship until 1956. *Agapenor*, built by Scotts at Greenock, became trapped in the Great Bitter Lake, Suez during the Six Day War between Egypt and Israel in 1967. *Anchises* was bombed by Chinese Nationalist aircraft on the Wangpoo River on 21 June 1949 and was later towed to Japan where she was repaired.

Peleus was built by Cammell Laird at Birkenhead in 1949. She was a steam turbine vessel with a service speed of 18 knots which enabled her to sail non-stop from Europe to Singapore in twenty days. *Pyrrhus* was nearly lost by fire at Liverpool in 1964. It took a full day to control the blaze and she was later repaired and continued in service.

In 1951 Elder Dempster purchased the fleet of ten ships owned by Henderson's British & Burmese Steam Navigation Co. and in 1953 the name of Elder Dempster Lines Holdings was changed to Liner Holdings. On 1 January 1965 the Ocean Steam Ship Co. acquired all the ordinary shares in Liner Holdings and later that year they also acquired the Guinea Gulf Line.

The Helenus class was designed with significant refrigerated cargo space for the Australian market. *Helenus* was built in 1949 and was followed by *Jason* and *Hector* in 1950 and *Ixion* in 1951. *Nestor*, *Theseus* and *Neleus* were followed by the first of the M-class vessels *Menelaus* in 1957. *Melampus* was trapped in the Great Bitter Lake in 1967 together with *Agapenor*. They were released from the Suez Canal in 1975 and later sold by the insurer to Greek and Panamanian owners.

The first Blue Funnel ship at the new berths at Vittoria Dock, Birkenhead.

A unique vessel was delivered to the Blue Funnel Line in 1964. *Centaur* was built at John Brown's yard on the Clyde for the Singapore to Fremantle service and was able to carry 190 passengers and 4,500 sheep.

Priam was built in 1966 and was the first of the final class of vessels to be designed and built for the Blue Funnel Line. They were handed over at the start of the container revolution and had a very short life with the company. *Priam*, *Peisander*, *Prometheus* and *Protesilaus* were sold to the C.Y. Tung Orient Overseas Line in 1979. Four other vessels of the Priam class were allocated to the Glen Line as *Radnorshire*, *Glenfinlas*, *Pembrokeshire* and *Glenalmond*.

A major financial commitment to new loading berths and facilities was completed at Vittoria Dock at Birkenhead in 1967. This complex was built in conjunction with the Mersey Docks & Harbour Board and cost £1.5 million. Blue Funnel Line were operating eight sailings a month from Birkenhead to the Far East when these new berths were opened and claimed that this was the most modern dock in Europe.

The name of Alfred Holt & Co. was changed to Ocean Fleets Ltd in 1967 and in 1972 the ships became the responsibility of various divisions of Ocean Transport & Trading Co.. They became the outright owners of the Elder Dempster and Paddy Henderson Lines in 1965 and bought the Guinea Gulf Line. Ships were regularly transferred between lines in this period and traditional Blue Funnel ships were seen in West African ports. The Palm Line was acquired from Unilever in 1984.

Maron, 1980, Blue Funnel Line, 16,482grt, 165m by 26m, 18 knots. She became *Studland Bay* in 1981, *Maron* in 1983, *Baltic Adventurer* in 1987, *Rainbow Avenue* and *Merchant Patriot* in 1988, *CMB Enterprise* in 1989, *Woermann Ubangi* in 1990, *Merchant Patriot* in 1991, *Lanka Amitha* in 1992 and finally *Merchant Patriot* again in 1994. On 30 December 1997 she was in danger of sinking in position 28.30N 75.48W as a ruptured seawater pipe had flooded the engine room and heavy seas were making progress impossible. The crew of twenty-eight were taken off by the US Coast Guard and she was towed to Freeport where she arrived on 5 January 1998. She was sold to Demeresa of Mexico for breaking up, which commenced on 25 June 1998.

Mentor, 1945, Blue Funnel Line, 7,642grt, 139m by 19m, 15½ knots. She was built as *Carthage Victory* and became *Mentor* in 1947, *Vita* in 1967, *Syra* in 1969. She was broken up in Split in 1971.

In November 1964 a serious fire broke out on the Blue Funnel cargo vessel *Pyrrhus* (1949/10,093grt) while she was unloading cargo at Liverpool. Firefighters took nearly twenty-four hours to control the blaze and the ship was at risk of capsizing on several occasions. *Pyrrhus* was repaired and gave the line a further eight years service. She was sold for demolition at Kaohsiung in 1972.

The Company was involved in the creation of Overseas Containers Ltd (OCL) which was taken over by P&O in 1986 and built several bulk carriers and tankers in 1971-75 as part of a diversification policy when it became clear that the traditional cargo trade was in decline .

In the 1970s the company had four container ships, *Menelaus*, *Memnon*, *Menetheus* and *Melampus*, built in Japanese yards and went back to Scotts at Greenock for the last class of vessels to be built for them. *Maron*, *Mentor* and *Myrmidon* had a very short life with the Ocean Group and were sold for further trading before the end of the 1980s. Palm Line, owned by Unilever, was bought in 1984. *Barber Perseus* and *Barber Hector* were built as the Ocean Group's contribution towards the Barber Blue Sea consortium from which they withdrew in 1988. The Elder Dempster Line, Palm Line and the Guinea Gulf Lines were sold to the French company Societe Navale Chargeurs Delmas-Vieljeux (SNCDV) in 1989.

When *Memnon* arrived at Falmouth in April 1989 for inspection prior to sale to the Pacific International Line, the Ocean Transport & Trading Co. moved out of deep-sea trading to concentrate in offshore operations. By 1996 Cory Towage had a fleet of fifty-six tugs operating in fourteen ports in the United Kingdom, Ireland and Canada and, under contract, in Angola and Panama. The offshore business had an established presence in the North Sea, West Africa, South East Asia, Brazil, India and the Middle East.

The Group reported a pre-tax profit of £83.1 million in 1998, which was up by 13% on the 1997 profit of £73.5 million. New contracts were gained in Oman and Venezuela but progress in the United Kingdom business was only satisfactory in overall terms.

Consequently, it came as no surprise that the Group had finally withdrawn from owning ships early in 2000. It sold Cory Towage to the Dutch company Wijsmuller for £81.8 million. Ocean said that the sale would enable it to develop its logistics and waste management activities of Cory Environment, which operates landfill disposal of waste and municipal services, such as refuse collection and street cleaning.

Ocean Group plc and the National Freight Corporation merged in 2000 to form Exel plc creating the world's second largest logistic group. It brought together Ocean Groups strengths in transporting goods internationally by air and sea freight with NFL's expertise in handling supply chains on the ground. The groups had complimentary customer bases, with Ocean being strong in healthcare and technology and NFL in automotive, chemical and retail sectors. The chief executive of the Ocean Group, John Allan, said that Exel would be able to manage entire chains from raw material sourcing to delivery to the customer. Gerry Murphy, chief executive of the National Frieght Corporation described it as a merger of equals and predicted it would generate £15 million of savings within two years.

The new company would have sales of £3.5 million and would handle logistics for around 70 per cent of the world's top 250 companies. The company was debt free and planned to expand its sea freight operations. NFL's John Devaney and David Finch became chairman and chief financial officer of Exel and Ocean's chairman Nigel Rich became deputy chairman. Exel plc acquired Tibbett & Britten, a leading British contract logistics business for $710 million and Deutsche Post took over Exel in December 2005. On completion of the deal Deutsche Post added DHL Express to operate as DHL Exel Supply Chain.

| VESSEL | Sails | | Arrive | | | | | | | | 10th NOVEMBER |
	Liverpool	Port Said	Penang	Port Swettenham	Singapore	Bangkok	Manila	Hong Kong	Kobe	Yokohama	Shanghai
AGAPENOR	11 Nov.	30 Nov.	4 Dec.	—	7 Dec.	14 Dec.	25 Dec.	21 Dec.	—	—	—
LAERTES	18 Nov.	27 Nov.	11 Dec.	13 Dec.	16 Dec.	—	—	22 Dec.	28 Dec.	31 Dec.	—
MEMNON H	19 Nov.	2 Dec.	—	—	16 Dec.	22 Dec.	29 Dec.	—	—	—	4 Jan.
LYCAON F	24 Nov.	3 Dec.	17 Dec.	19 Dec.	22 Dec.	—	—	28 Dec.	3 Jan.	—	—
ANTENOR	1 Dec.	10 Dec.	23 Dec.	25 Dec.	28 Dec.	—	—	3 Jan.	—	—	—
PYRRHUS H	7 Dec.	11 Dec.	—	—	—	—	9 Jan.	14 Jan.	20 Jan.	23 Jan.	—
AENEAS J	8 Dec.	17 Dec.	2 Jan.	4 Jan.	7 Jan.	—	—	14 Jan.	—	—	—
MELAMPUS	10 Dec.	19 Dec.	—	—	2 Jan.	9 Jan.	20 Jan.	16 Jan.	—	—	—
AJAX P	19 Dec.	28 Dec.	10 Jan.	12 Jan.	15 Jan.	—	—	21 Jan.	27 Jan.	30 Jan.	—
MARON HL	20 Dec.	2 Jan.	—	—	16 Jan.	22 Jan.	1 Feb.	—	—	—	6 Feb.
ANCHISES	23 Dec.	1 Jan.	15 Jan.	17 Jan.	20 Jan.	—	—	26 Jan.	1 Feb.	—	—
EUMAEUS	31 Dec.	9 Jan.	23 Jan.	25 Jan.	28 Jan.	—	—	3 Feb.	—	—	—
PELEUS H	7 Jan.	21 Jan.	—	—	—	—	9 Feb.	14 Feb.	20 Feb.	23 Feb.	—
TELEMACHUS J	7 Jan.	16 Jan.	1 Feb.	3 Feb.	8 Feb.	—	—	—	—	—	—
ACHILLES	11 Jan.	20 Jan.	—	—	3 Feb.	10 Feb.	21 Feb.	17 Feb.	—	—	—
ADRASTUS F	18 Jan.	27 Jan.	10 Feb.	12 Feb.	15 Feb.	—	—	21 Feb.	27 Feb.	2 Mar.	—
CYCLOPS HL	20 Jan.	2 Feb.	—	—	17 Feb.	23 Feb.	5 Mar.	—	—	—	10 Mar.
POLYDORUS	24 Jan.	2 Feb.	16 Feb.	18 Feb.	21 Feb.	—	—	27 Feb.	5 Mar.	—	—
AUTOLYCUS	1 Feb.	10 Feb.	24 Feb.	26 Feb.	1 Mar.	—	—	—	7 Mar.	—	—

Scheduled sailing list for 1967.

Theseus, 1955, Blue Funnel Line, 7,803grt, 149m by 20m, 16 knots. She was sold in 1971 becoming *Aegis Myth*, then *Aegis Care* in 1972 and broken up in Shanghai, China in 1973.

Menestheus, 1958, Blue Funnel Line, 8,510grt, 151m by 20m, 16½knots. She became *Onitsha* in 1977, *Elisland* in 1978 and broken up at Kaohsiung in 1979.

ESCOMBE. McGRATH & CO. LTD. LIVERPOOL.

FORTNIGHTLY SHIPPING LIST.

IMPORTANT.—Shippers must **NOT** despatch cargo to any vessels until receipt of Calling Forward Notice from us.

PORT	STEAMER	Approx. date of Closing	LINE	Loading at
CALCUTTA	Maskeliya	Jan. 7	Brocklebank	Birkenhead
	Mandasor	Jan. 17	Brocklebank	Birkenhead
BOMBAY	City of Agra	Jan. 6	Hall	Birkenhead
	Caledonia	Jan. 6	Anchor	Birkenhead
	Indian Trust	Jan. 13	India	Birkenhead
	City of Singapore	Jan. 18	City	Birkenhead
KARACHI	City of Agra	Jan. 6	Hall	Birkenhead
	Indian Trust	Jan. 13	India	Birkenhead
	City of Singapore	Jan. 18	City	Birkenhead
MADRAS	Steamer	Mid Jan.		Birkenhead
COLOMBO	Derbyshire	Jan. 3	Bibby	Birkenhead
	Clan Cumming	Jan. 18	Clan	Birkenhead
RANGOON	Derbyshire	Jan 3	Bibby	Birkenhead
	Salween	Jan. 17	Henderson	Birkenhead
SINGAPORE, BANGKOK, HONG KONG, MANILA	Automedon	Jan. 6	Holt	Birkenhead
PENANG, PRAI, PORT SWETTENHAM, SINGAPORE, HONG KONG, JAPAN, PUSAN	Adrastus	Jan. 13	Holt	Birkenhead
SINGAPORE, BANGKOK LABUAN, MANILA, SHANGHAI	Achilles	Jan. 17	Holt	Birkenhead
PENANG, PRAI, PORT SWETTENHAM, SINGAPORE, HONG KONG, KOBE	Polydorus	Jan. 19	Holt	Birkenhead
INDONESIA	Cyclops	Jan. 24	Holt	Birkenhead
PENANG, PRAI, PORT SWETTENHAM, SINGAPORE, HONG KONG, HSINKANG	Autolycus	Jan. 27	Holt	Birkenhead
AUSTRALIA　　Fremantle, Adelaide, Melbourne	*Rhexenor	Jan. 6	Gracie	Liverpool
†Sydney, Brisbane	†Middlesex	Jan. 13	Marwood	Liverpool
‡Fremantle, Melbourne, Adelaide	‡Nottingham	Jan. 13	Marwood	Liverpool
NEW ZEALAND　Auckland, Wellington, Lyttelton Dunedin	Suffolk	Jan. 13	Dowie	Liverpool
EAST AFRICA	City of Chester	Jan. 11	Staveley	Birkenhead
	Author	Jan. 25	Staveley	Birkenhead
LA GUAIRA, PUERTO CABELLO, CURACAO, MARACAIBO	Diplomat	Jan. 6	Harrison	Liverpool
	Crofter	Jan. 20	Harrison	Liverpool
TRINIDAD & BARBADOS	Diplomat	Jan. 10	Harrison	Liverpool
	Suninger	Jan. 16	Saguenay	Liverpool
KINGSTON & MEXICO	Wayfarer	Jan. 3	Harrison	Liverpool
	Defender	Jan. 17	Harrison	Liverpool
DEMERARA	Suninger	Jan. 16	Saguenay	Liverpool
	Arakaka	Jan. 17	Booker	Liverpool
COLOMBIA, ECUADOR, PERU & CHILE	Flamenco	Jan. 7	P.S.N.C.	Liverpool
PERU & CHILE	Santander	Jan. 16	P.S.N.C.	Liverpool
DURBAN, LOURENCO MARQUES, BEIRA	Tribesman	Jan. 10	Staveley	Birkenhead
	Constantia	Jan. 17	S.A.F. Marine	Birkenhead
	Argyllshire	Jan. 20	Clan	Birkenhead
CAPE TOWN, PT. ELIZABETH EAST LONDON　*Takes Lobito & Mauritius	Clan Macintyre	Jan. 3	Clan	Birkenhead
	*Clan Sutherland	Jan. 13	Clan	Birkenhead
	Factor	Jan. 24	Staveley	Birkenhead

OTHER PORTS. Particulars can be obtained upon application to us.

Escombe McGrath fortnightly shipping list, December 1960.

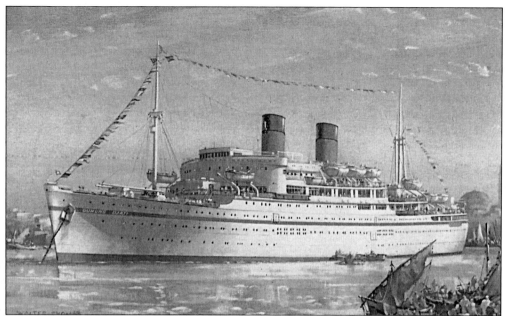

Blue Funnel Line. *Gunung Djati* was built as the *Pretoria* by Blohm & Voss, Hamburg, for the East Africa Line. She became a German Navy accommodation ship in 1939 and in 1945 was taken over by Britain and renamed *Empire Doon*. In 1949 she was renamed *Empire Orwell* and was employed as a troopship by the Ministry of Transport. She was bought by Alfred Holt in 1958 and converted into a Pilgrim ship to carry 106 first class passengers and 2,000 third class. She was sold to the Indonesian Government in 1962 and purchased by P.T. Maskapai Pelajaran 'Sang Saka' in 1965 and P.T. Perusahaan Pelajaran in 1966. A Pakistan firm bought her in 1968. She became an Indonesian Navy accommodation ship in 1980 renamed *Kri Tanjung Pandam* and was broken up in 1987.

Crosby Dale (1927/213grt) was originally the *Xanthus*. She became *Crosby Dale* in 1959, owned by T. Routledge and was broken up at Dalmuir in 1968.

Centaur, 1964, Blue Funnel Line, 8,262grt, 146m by 20m, 20 knots. She became *Hai Long* in 1985 and *Hai Da* in 1986.

Peisander, 1967, Blue Funnel Line, 12,094grt, 172m by 24m, 21 knots. In 1979 *Peisander* was renamed *Oriental Exporter*, *Main Exporter* in 1981 and *Oriental Exporter* in 1984. She was broken up at Kaohsiung in 1986.

Priam, 1966, Blue Funnel Line, 12,094grt, 172m by 24m, 21knots. She became *Oriental Champion* in 1979. On 18 October 1985 she was disabled by an Iraqi missile and was towed to Bahrain for inspection. As it was uneconomical to repair the damage, she was broken up at Kaohsiung later that year.

Polyphemus, 1948, Blue Funnel Line, 7,401grt, 148m by 19m, 15 knots. *Polyphemus* was built as *Achilles* and became *Radnorshire* in 1949, *Asphalion* in 1963, *Polyphemus* in 1966, *Asphalion* again in 1972 and *Gulf Anchor* in 1975. She was broken up at Kaohsiung in 1979.

Breconshire, 1942, Glen Line, 9,061grt, 156m by 20m, 17 knots. She was launched as *HMS Activity* and became *Breconshire* in 1946. She was broken up at Etajima Island, near Kure in 1967.

Glenalmond, 1966, Glen Line, 12,299grt, 173m by 23m, 20 knots. She became the *Patroclus* in 1973 and the *Rajab I* in 1982. On 18 July 1984 she arrived at Port Rashid on fire, which had started on a voyage from Bangkok to Dubai. It took four days to extinguish the fire and she was sold for demolition at Gadani Beach because it was uneconomical to repair her

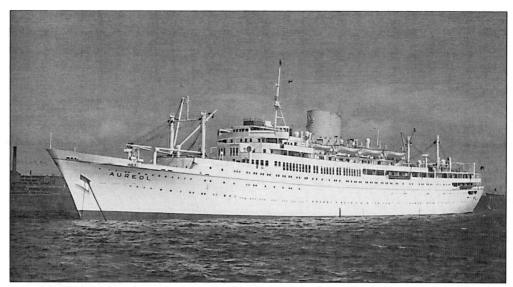

Aureol (1951/14,083grt) was built on the River Clyde and sailed on her maiden voyage from Liverpool to Apapa on 3 November, 1951. In 1972 passenger services were transferred to Southampton and she took the last sailing from Liverpool on 16 March that year. She was laid up in Southampton in 1974 when she was sold to Marianna Shipping & Trading Co. for use as an accommodation vessel at Jeddah. She was renamed *Marianna VI*. She was moved to Eleusis, Greece in 1991 where she was laid up for over ten years. On 5 June 2001 she arrived at Alang where she was broken up.

Accra (1947/11,644grt) was built by Vickers Armstrong at Barrow-in-Furness for Elder Dempster's Liverpool-Lagos service. She and her sister *Apapa* were originally painted with black hulls but these were changed to grey in 1949. On 8 November 1967 she left Liverpool to be broken up in Cartegena, Spain.

Owerri, 1955, Elder Dempster Line, 6,240grt, 137m by 19m, 12½ knots. She was renamed *Maldive Courage* in 1972 and broken up at Gadani Beach in 1983.

Onitsha, 1952, Elder Dempster Line, 5,802grt, 137m by 18m, 11 knots. She was renamed *Amvourgon* in 1972. On a voyage from Quebec to Baltimore, 8 January 1975, she suffered a serious engine room fire and was abandoned. She was towed to Halifax and then to Santander in May that year to be broken up.

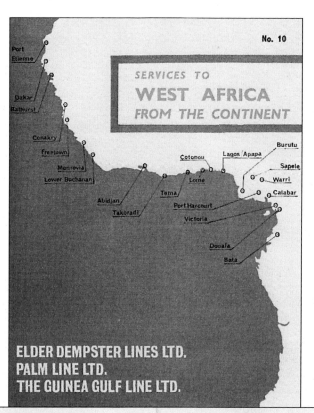

SERVICES TO
WEST AFRICA
FROM THE CONTINENT

Port Etienne
Dakar
Bathurst
Conakry
Freetown
Monrovia
Lower Buchanan
Abidjan
Takoradi
Tema
Lome
Cotonou
Lagos Apapa
Burutu
Sapele
Warri
Calabar
Port Harcourt
Victoria
Douala
Bata

ELDER DEMPSTER LINES LTD.
PALM LINE LTD.
THE GUINEA GULF LINE LTD.

		ELDER DEMPSTER LINES, LIMITED, LIVERPOOL				PALM LINE LIMITED, LONDON							

No. 10
Southbound Sailings

CONTINENT/WEST AFRICA

VESSEL		Bremen	Hamburg	Antwerp	Rotterdam	Dakar	Bathurst	Conakry	Freetown	Monrovia	Abidjan	Takoradi	Tema
KOYAN	(Elder)		18 Sept.	21 Sept.	24 Sept.	26 Sept.							
FOURAH BAY	(R) (Elder)		Ø	28 Sept.	1 Oct.	3 Oct.				11 Oct.			14 Oct.	16 Oct.
DONGA	(R) (Elder)	Rostock 30 Sept.	2 Oct.	1 Oct.	5 Oct.	8 Oct.	16 Oct.	17 Oct.	20 Oct.		22 Oct.	29 Oct.	31 Oct.	3 Nov.
DUMURRA	(R) (Elder)		2 Oct.	5 Oct.	8 Oct.	10 Oct.							
LOBITO PALM	(R) (Palm)		Ø	12 Oct.	15 Oct.	17 Oct.				25 Oct.			28 Oct.	30 Oct.
BADAGRY PALM	(R) (Palm)		16 Oct.	19 Oct.	22 Oct.	24 Oct.							
FLORENCE HOLT	(Gulf)		Ø	26 Oct.	29 Oct.	31 Oct.				8 Nov.			11 Nov.	13 Nov.
NIGER PALM	(Palm)	Stettin 26 Oct.	30 Oct.	29 Oct.	2 Nov.	5 Nov.	14 Nov.	15 Nov.		21 Nov.			24 Nov.	27 Nov.
AKASSA PALM	(R) (Palm)		30 Oct.	2 Nov.	5 Nov.	7 Nov.							
DUNKWA	(R) (Elder)		Ø	9 Nov.	12 Nov.	14 Nov.				22 Nov.			25 Nov.	27 Nov.
VESSEL	(Elder)	Stettin 9 Nov.	13 Nov.	12 Nov.	16 Nov.	19 Nov.	28 Nov.	29 Nov.		5 Dec.			8 Dec.	11 Dec.
LAGOS PALM	(R) (Palm)		13 Nov.	16 Nov.	19 Nov.	21 Nov.							
FALABA	(R) (Elder)		Ø	23 Nov.	26 Nov.	28 Nov.				6 Dec.			9 Dec.	11 Dec.
VESSEL			23 Nov.	26 Nov.	30 Nov.	3 Dec.	12 Dec.	13 Dec.	16 Dec.	19 Dec.	26 Dec.		

HAMBURG
Elderpalm Schiffahrts—Agentur G.m.b.H.
Schaartor 1, 11.
Tel: 36 29 01

BREMEN
Herm. Dauelsberg,
P.O. Box 23
Tel. 31 671

For details of Cargo Bookings, Through Bill of Lading Services and for General information, application should be made to the booking agents.

Cargo will be accepted for other ports subject to special arrangement.

Cargo to Harbel is accepted on Through Bill of Lading via Monrovia

*If Sufficient Inducement

(R) Vessels fitted with Refrigerator Space

* Limited quantity only

‡ These vessels will serve Lower Buchanan, Sinoe, Cape Palmas, subject to sufficient inducement.

Ø Cargo from Bremen accepted with transhipment at Hamburg

Elder Dempster, Palm Line and Guinea Gulf Line sailing lists, 24 September 1963.

Donga, 1960, Elder Dempster Line, 6,565grt, 142m by 19m, 14 knots. She was renamed *Diamant Merchant* in 1981 and broken up at Alang, where she arrived on 7 October 1983.

Mamfe, 1947, Elder Dempster Line, 4,810grt, 124m by 17m, 12 knots. She was built as *Salaga* and renamed *Mamfe* in 1965. She became *Lucky Trader* in 1968 and was broken up in Hsinkang, China in 1973.

Kalaw, 1959, British & Burmese S.N. Co., 5,445grt, 139m by 18m, 11 knots. She was built as the *Pradsu*, renamed *Kalaw* in 1964 and *Kohima* in 1966. She was broken up at Kaohsiung in 1973.

Makurdi Palm, 1953, Palm Line, 6,178grt, 131m by 17m, 12 knots. She was built as the *Tema Palm*, becoming *Makurdi Palm* in 1960 and *Santamar* in 1969. She was broken up in 1976.

Three

Ellerman Lines

City of Bristol, 1945, Ellerman Lines, 7,096grt, 137m by 18m, 14 knots. She was built as *Sacramento* and renamed *City of Bristol* in 1964, *Felicie* in 1969 and *30 De Noviembre* in 1970. She was broken up at Faslane in 1977.

City of Khartoum, 1946, Ellerman Lines, 9,955grt, 152m by 20m, 14½knots. She was sold to the Ben Line in 1968 and renamed *Benalligin*. She was broken up at Kaohsiung in 1972.

City of Liverpool, 1949, Ellerman Lines, 7,612grt, 148m by 19m, 15 knots. She was sold in 1967 and renamed *Kavo Grossos*. She left Singapore on 16 January 1973, arriving at Shanghai on 5 February for demolition.

In 1892 John Reeves Ellerman became the Managing Director of Frederick Leyland & Co. Ltd after the sudden death of Frederick Leyland. He used his financial expertise and joined with Christopher Furness and Henry O'Hagan to purchase the fleet of the Leyland Line. The following year he became Chairman of the company and negotiated various deals to take over collieries which provided coal to fuel the Line's vessels.

He sold the North Atlantic aspects of the Leyland Line to the American financier J. Pierpont Morgan in 1901 but kept the Mediterranean, Portugese, Antwerp and Montreal parts of the business. Twenty ships were retained by Ellerman and eight purchased from Nicholas Papayanni at a cost of £132,850.

The London, Liverpool & Ocean Shipping Co. was formed, which operated the twenty-eight ships to ports in the Mediterranean. Half the shares in the City Line and Hall Line were acquired in 1901, increasing the fleet by twenty six ships owned by the two lines and the name was changed to Ellerman Lines. In 1902 the fleet of William Wescott & Laurence was added providing the company with services from London.

An agreement was negotiated with T.&J. Harrison and the Clan Line to enter into the South African trade in 1902. A joint service to South America was agreed with the Allan Line in 1903 and an interest in the Glen Lines services in the Far East Conference was obtained by the Line in 1905. The Bucknall Steamship Lines were taken over in 1908 and the name of the company was changed to the Ellerman & Bucknall Steamship Co. in 1914 when they joined the Far East Conference and the Rangoon Homeward Conference.

When Thomas Wilson, Sons & Co. was taken over in 1916 by John Ellerman, the name changed to Ellerman's Wilson Line. The West Hartlepool firm of shipbuilders of William Grey was part purchased to enable the fleet to be rebuilt following the end of the First World War. Montgomerie & Workmen, the London agents, were acquired in 1920.

The Ellerman and Papayanni services were merged in 1932 to become Ellerman & Papayanni Lines and in the Great Depression of the early 1930s the Ellerman Lines expanded their services. When Sir John Reeves Ellerman died in 1933, Sir Miles Mattinson became chairman of the company and the fleet of five vessels owned by Montgomerie & Workman were incorporated into the Ellerman fleet in 1936.

Ellerman Lines joined with the New Zealand Shipping Co. and Port Line in 1936 to provide a service from New Zealand and Australia to ports on the Eastern Seaboard of the United States and Canada between Galveston, Charleston and Montreal. They were joined by Shaw Savill & Albion in 1957 when the service was renamed the Crusader Shipping Co..

In the Second World War, Ellerman Lines lost fifty-eight ships. The *City of Benares* was 480 miles north west of Ireland on 17 September 1940 when she was torpedoed and sunk by U-48. She was sailing from Liverpool to Canada, carrying 406 passengers and crew. Only 150 people survived this tragedy.

A rebuilding programme was authorized on the cessation of hostilities. However, on 15 August 1947, India and Pakistan achieved independence and announced plans to set up their own merchant fleets. This had an immediate consequence on the fortunes of the Group and saw the start in the decline of numbers of ships in the fleet. In 1950 South Africa Lines and South African Marine joined the South African Conference, the Burmese services were withdrawn in 1952 and the passenger services to India ceased in 1953. The Pakistan Steamship Lines joined the India Conference in 1960 and in the following year the United States to India service was withdrawn.

Ellerman's Wilson Line began a joint service with Swedish Lloyd using roll-on, roll-off ferries between Hull to Gothenburg in 1964. Ellerman & Papayanni converted the *Catanian*

City of Hull, 1971, Ellerman Lines, 9,767grt, 153m by 22m, 18 knots. She became the *St John* in 1980, *Seagull* in 1982, *Sea Lady* in 1985 and *Magdalena* in 1996. She arrived at Alang on 28 August 1996 for breaking up.

City of Bath, 1947, Ellerman Lines, 7,030grt, 148m by 19m, 15 knots. She was built as *Langleescot* and became *City of Bath* in 1952, *Lena* in 1969 and was broken up in 1972.

and the *Malatian* to carry containers and chartered the *Cortian* in 1966 for the Lisbon service. Ellerman, Blue Star Line, Port Line and Australian National Line formed Associated Container Transportation (Australia) Ltd in 1967 to provide a container service.

From 1968 services to the Far East were operated by the joint Ellerman & Ben Line and in March 1969 a new container vessel, *ACT 1*, entered the Associated Container Transportation Line. The Ellerman & Papayanni service was containerized with the charter of Hustler class ships from Seacontainers and services transferred to Ellesmere Port from Liverpool in 1972.

A restructuring of the Group took place in 1973 when the Papayanni, Westcott & Laurence, Hall and Ellerman & Bucknall Lines vanished to be replaced by Ellerman City Liners. The container vessel *City of Edinburgh* came into service on 9 November 1973. Ellerman Lines had a share in the vessel although she was owned by the Ben Line. *City of Durban* entered service for the Ellerman-Harrison Container Line in 1978.

The Ellerman Group was sold for £9 million in 1983 and the remaining ships were re-registered in the Isle of Man in 1984. Although the fleet comprised six ships, only one was actually owned by Ellerman City Liners as the others were chartered from banks. There was a management buy-back in 1985 but the Line was purchased in 1987 for £24.1 million by Trafalgar House, who already owned the Cunard Line. A new freight operation was formed under the name of Cunard-Ellerman with a fleet of nineteen ships.

On 14 October 1991, the P&O Steam Navigation Co. bought the Ellerman shipping and container interests from Trafalgar House for £42.5 million. Sixteen vessels were involved and Trafalgar House retained the Cunard name. The Mediterranean, Middle East, Indian and East African interests in the Cunard-Ellerman Group were sold to Andrew Weir Shipping Ltd (The Bank Line).

P&O took over the container ships *ACT 1*, *ACT 2* and *ACT 7*, which were jointly owned by the Blue Star Line, Port Line and Ellerman Lines, *City of Durban* owned by Ellerman Lines and the Charente Steam Ship Co. (T&J Harrison Ltd), *New Zealand Mariner*, *New Zealand Pacific*, and the tanker *Lumiere*. Blue Star Line took over *ACT 3*, *ACT 4*, *ACT 5*, *ACT 6* and *ACT 10*, which were all jointly owned by the Blue Star Line, Port Line and the Ellerman Lines.

Andrew Weir Shipping took over four of Ellerman Lines' container ships *City of Manchester*, *City of Plymouth*, *Liverpool Star* and *Oxford*, and the deal did not affect the Atlantic Container Line's vessel *Atlantic Conveyor*.

In 2003 the Andrew Weir Shipping Group sold Ellerman Lines to the Hamburg Sud Group. This included the services to the Mediterranean and to India and Pakistan. However, the Ellerman name was replaced by the Hamburg Sud name in 2005, and another famous shipping line disappeared.

City of Canberra, 1961, Ellerman Lines, 10,543grt, 156m by 20m, 17½ knots. She was sold in 1977, renamed *Tasgold* and broken up at Kaohsiung in 1980.

Benratha (1956/7,727grt) was built as the *City of Newcastle*. She was chartered to Ben Line and renamed in 1968. When the charter terminated in 1971, she reverted to *City of Newcastle*. She was sold in 1978 and renamed *Eastern Envoy* and arrived at Chittagong for demolition on 23 October 1980.

City of Chicago, 1950, Ellerman Lines, 7,622grt, 148m by 19m, 15 knots. She was laid down as *City of Bath*. She became *Kaptamarco* in 1967, *Marco* in 1970 and broken up in Shanghai in 1971.

City of Pretoria (1947/8,450grt) prepares to sail from Birkenhead. She was renamed *Proxeneion* in 1967 and broken up in Japan later that year.

City of Port Elizabeth, 1952, Ellerman Lines, 13,363grt, 165m by 22m, 16½knots. She was sold in 1971 becoming *Mediterranean Island* and later *Mediterranean Sun*. She was broken up at Kaohsiung in 1980.

City of Coventry, 1949, Ellerman Lines, 7,568grt, 148m by 19m, 15 knots. She was renamed *Ingrid* in 1967, *Annie* in 1969 and arrived at Kaohsiung on 5 June 1970 for breaking up.

Island of Marmara, 1960, 7,155grt, 132m by 18m, 14 knots. She was built as the Ellerman cargo vessel *City of St Albans* and became *Island of Marmara* in 1979. She was broken up at Jamnagar in 1983.

City of Liverpool, 1970, Ellerman Lines, 9,767grt, 153m by 22m, 18 knots. She was sold in 1981, renamed *Marianthe*, and was broken up at Kaohsiung in 1986.

Arcadian, 1960, Ellerman & Papayanni Lines, 3,402grt, 112m by 16m, 13½knots. She became *City of Famagusta* in 1974, *Batroun* in 1977 and arrived at Gadani Beach on 18 December 1986 for breaking up.

Crosbian, 1947, Ellerman & Papayanni Lines, 1,518grt, 83m by 13m, 12 knots. She was renamed *Mabuhay* in 1967 and broken up in Manila in 1980.

Malatian, 1958, Ellerman & Papayanni Lines, 1,407grt, 82m by 13m, 12 knots. She became *Maldive Victory* in 1971. On 13 February 1981, she was stranded on a reef and sank at the entrance to Male on a voyage from Singapore.

Cortian, 1962, Ellerman & Papayanni Lines, 537grt, 71m by 10m, 11 knots. She was built as *Cortia* and renamed *Cortian* in 1966, reverting back to *Cortia* in 1971, *Austerity* in 1974, *Bruno Alphina* in 1978 and *Siba Foggia* in 1986. On a voyage from Jeddah to Trieste on 4 December 1994, she was abandoned after taking on water and three crew were lost. The vessel remained afloat and was towed to Limassol where she arrived on 7 December. She was towed to Vassilikis on 10 March 1995 for repairs and sold in 1996, becoming *Nehmet Allah* and, *Fighter 11* in 1998.

City of Dublin (1983/17,414grt) is presently operating in Ellerman Line colours on charter to Andrew Weir Shipping. She was built as *Corona* and has had a number of names including *City of London* and *City of Antwerp*.

City of Glasgow (1978/14,050grt) was built as *Alltrans Express*, becoming *TFL Express* in 1980, *Nedlloyd Express* and *Express* in 1986, *Zim Guam* in 1988 and *City of Glasgow* in 1998.

Four

Cayzer, Irvine & Co.

Clan Macdonald, 1939, Clan Line, 8,141grt, 154m by 20m, 14 knots. She was broken up in 1970.

Clan Mactaggart, 1949, Clan Line, 8,035grt, 154m by 20m, 16 knots. She was broken up at Bilbao, Spain in 1971.

Charles Cayzer bought two sailing ships in 1877 to provide a service from Liverpool to Bombay. He was joined by Captain William Irvine who was an experienced mariner. Capital for the venture was obtained from Alexander Stephen of Linthouse, Glasgow, and the firm of Cayzer, Irvine was established in Liverpool.

The new company's first ship *Clan Alpine* was launched on 16 September 1878 at Alexander Stephen's yard on the River Clyde. She was the first of a class of six ships which were in service between Glasgow, Liverpool and India. The following year. William Irvine died leaving Charles Cayzer to run the business.

A service from Glasgow to South Africa was introduced in 1881 and the Clan Line of Steamers Ltd was formed in 1890 with Charles Cayzer holding the controlling interest. Services from Manchester were provided in 1895 and ships were built for new services to East Africa, Mauritius, Chittagong and Buenos Aires at the end of the nineteenth century.

In 1918 the Scottish Shire Line, who provided refrigerated meat services from Australia and New Zealand, and the Houston Lines services to South America were taken over. The end of the First World War brought a rebuilding programme and a relationship with the Greenock Dockyard which was to last for many years. The line eventually purchased the shipyard in 1930 and built twenty-four Clan Macarthur type ships.

Thirty-six ships were lost during the Second World War and, as a temporary measure, standard Liberty, Ocean and Empire vessels were brought into service for the line. New vessels started to enter service with the launch of the *Clan Mactaggart* on 8 October 1948 and *Clan Shaw* sailing on her maiden voyage from Birkenhead on 25 January 1950. Scottish Tankers was formed in 1952 and *Scottish Lion* and *Scottish Eagle* entered service.

Kenya Castle (1952/17,041grt) was built for Union Castle Line's Round Africa service. She left London on her maiden voyage on 4 April 1952. In 1959 she had her funnel height increased and a dome fitted to the top. She arrived to lay up on the River Fal on 22 April 1967, and later that year she was sold to Chandris Lines and renamed *Amerikanis*. Her maiden voyage for Chandris Line was on 8 August 1968 when she left Piraeus for New York. She became a very successful and popular cruise liner in their fleet, and continued in that role until she was withdrawn and broken up at Alang in 2001.

In 1955 British & Commonwealth Shipping Ltd was formed with the merger of Clan and Union Castle lines. The Union Castle Line originated from the Union Line steamer *Dane*, which carried the line's first Royal Mail from Southampton to Cape Town on 15 September 1857. Services were extended to Durban and Port Elizabeth in the 1860s and their monopoly was challenged in 1870 when the Cape & Natal Line was established by George H. Payne, a South African businessman.

Payne chartered two Currie Line steamers in 1872 but because of financial problems he asked Donald Currie of the Castle Line to take over the service to Cape Town. Currie decided to concentrate his energy on his South African services and abandoned his services to India. The South African Shipping Conference was set up in 1883 with the Union Line, Aberdeen Line, Bullard King and Clan Line.

In 1891 the Union Line and Castle Line made Southampton the main port for their South African services. The Union Line vessel *Scot* sailed in July and *Dunottar Castle* sailed for the Castle Line to Cape Town in September 1891. On 8 March 1900 the merger between the Union Line and the Castle Line took place.

The Union Castle Line started a monthly intermediate service between London, Cape Town and Mombasa, and the Round Africa service from London and Southampton to Gibralter, Marseilles, Naples, Aden, Mombasa and Durban in 1910.

In December 1911 it was announced that the Royal Mail Line had made an offer for the Union Castle Line and this takeover occurred on 18 April 1912. The chairman of the company was Sir Owen Phillips, later Lord Kylsant, who was also chairman of the Elder Dempster Line, King Line, Royal Mail Line, Shire Line and the Pacific Steam Navigation Co. Following financial concerns in 1931, Lord Kylsant resigned from the board and was replaced by Robertson F. Gibb in 1932.

New ships were built in the 1930s and the mail contract was renewed for a ten-year period from 1937, with the stipulation that the passage time would be fourteen days. As only two of the line's ships could maintain this voyage time, a new rebuilding and refurbishment programme was approved by the Board. *Athlone Castle* was the first vessel to sail on the fourteen-day timetable when she left Southampton on 22 December 1938.

Following the Second World War a new mail contract was signed and in 1948 the *Pretoria Castle* sailed on her maiden voyage. She was followed into service that year by a sister ship *Edinburgh Castle*. The one-class vessel *Bloemfontain Castle* was introduced in 1950 for the East African service. *Rhodesia Castle*, *Kenya Castle* and *Braemar Castle* were built for the Round Africa service.

The South African-based Springbok Line was established in 1959 when some Clan Line vessels were transferred and given Bullard King names. By 1961 the Springbok Line was taken over by Safmarine and the ships were given names beginning with 'South African'.

Good Hope Castle and *Southampton Castle* were delivered in 1965. They were designed as fast cargo vessels to run alongside the mail ships, having a speed of 22½knots. Both ships were fitted with passenger accommodation in 1967 to allow a service to be provided to Ascension Island and St Helena.

Cayzer Irvine took over the management of the Bowater Steamship Co. in 1963 and the Greenock Dockyard was taken over by Scotts in 1966. The last ship to be built for the Clan Line, *Clan Alpine*, was delivered by Scotts of Greenock in April 1967.

The passenger and cargo vessels in the Union Castle fleet were gradually disposed of in the 1970s. *Riebeeck Castle*, *Roslin Castle* and *Rowallan Castle* were sold to the breakers in 1971 and *Tintagel Castle* and *Tantallon Castle* were also disposed of in 1971. *Edinburgh Castle* went to the ship-breakers in 1976 and *Pendennis Castle* was sold for further trading the same year.

Clan Ramsey and her three sisters, which had been completed in 1965-1966, were transferred to the Union Castle Line in 1976. The last passenger sailing by a Union Castle Line vessel from Southampton to Cape Town took place on 12 August 1977 by the mail ship *Windsor Castle*.

Clan Macgillivray, 1962, Clan Line, 9,039grt, 155m by 19m, 16½knots. She was sold in 1981 and renamed *Clan Macboyd* and broken up at Shanghai in 1984.

The Overseas Container Line and the Harrison Line ordered two container ships for the East African services, and British & Commonwealth Shipping purchased the Harrison Line vessel *Specialist* in 1976. *Good Hope Castle* and *Southampton Castle* were sold to Costa Armatori in 1978. A new joint service with Safmarine began in 1979 and the Clan Ramsey class lost their 'Castle' names which were substituted by 'Universal'.

By 1979 the Company's shipping services were operating at a loss. In November 1981 *Clan Macgregor* unloaded at Avonmouth and Manchester's Salford Dock. She was the last Clan Line ship in service and in 1982 became the *Angelika R. Clan Macgillivray*, berthed at Chittagong was sold at the same time, bringing to an end the history of one of Britain's major shipping lines.

CAMMELL LAIRD AND COMPANY (Shipbuilders & Engineers) LIMITED

LAUNCH OF
R.M.S. "WINDSOR CASTLE"
By Her Majesty
QUEEN ELIZABETH THE QUEEN MOTHER
On TUESDAY, 23rd JUNE, 1959.

ENTRANCE TO YARD, THE COMPOUND, NEW CHESTER ROAD
ADMIT ONE
TO
Green Enclosure

VISITORS SHOULD BE IN THEIR PLACES NOT LATER THAN 12-30 P.M.

FOR CONDITIONS SEE BACK

Entrance to the Works and the Green Enclosure will only be possible on presentation of this card.

NO SPACE FOR PARKING CARS AVAILABLE INSIDE THE WORKS.

Windsor Castle (1960/37,647grt) was launched by Her Majesty the Queen Mother at Cammell Laird's Shipyard, Birkenhead on 23 June 1959. She sailed from Southampton to Cape Town and Durban on 18 August 1960 on her maiden voyage. She took the final passenger sailing by the line on 12 August 1977 and was sold to the Greek shipowner John Latsis later that year and renamed *Margarita L*. She was converted to a luxury floating hotel for use at Jeddah. She remained there until 1991 when she returned to Piraeus, where she has since been laid up.

Pendennis Castle (1958/28,582grt) was built by Harland & Wolff at Belfast and sailed on her maiden voyage from Southampton on 1 January 1959. She continued in service until 1976 when she was sold to the Ocean Queen Navigation Corporation of Panama and renamed *Ocean Queen*. She was sold again in 1978, becoming *Sinbad I*. In 1980 she was broken up at Kaohsiung.

S.A.Vaal (1961/32,697grt) was built as the *Transvaal Castle* for the Union Castle Line service to the Cape. She was transferred to the South African Marine Corporation in 1966 and renamed *S.A.Vaal*. Her port of registry was changed to Cape Town in 1969 and she was sold to the Carnival Corporation in 1977 and renamed *Festivale*. With new tonnage being added to the Carnival fleet, she was disposed of in 1996 and renamed *Island Breeze*, and then *Big Red Boat III* in 2000.

UNION-CASTLE LINE
ROYAL MAIL SERVICE TO SOUTH AFRICA

R.M.M.V.

"STIRLING CASTLE"
(Berth 104)

Sailing from SOUTHAMPTON on Thursday, 16th MAY, is expected to take cargo arriving alongside up to the evening of Tuesday, 14th MAY for :—

				Arriving
MADEIRA	...	...	...	19 MAY
CAPE TOWN	...	...	...	30 MAY
PORT ELIZABETH	...	...	...	1 JUNE
EAST LONDON	...	...	...	3 JUNE
DURBAN	...	...	...	4 JUNE
MOSSEL BAY	...	...	...	9 JUNE

also by transhipment for Walvis Bay, Luderitz Bay, Lourenço Marques, Beira and Mauritius.

All Shippers are recommended to despatch cargo by Thursday, or not later than Friday, to ensure its arrival at Southampton by Monday at the latest.

Following Mail Sailings from Southampton :—

R.M.S. "WINDSOR CASTLE" ... *Thursday, 23rd MAY*
R.M.S. "PRETORIA CASTLE" ... *Thursday, 30th MAY*

GREENLY HOUSE,   AVENUE 4343
30, Creechurch Lane, E.C.3.
2nd May, 1963.

Stirling Castle (1936/25,554grt) was launched on 15 July 1935 by Mrs Robertson Gibb, wife of the Chairman of the Union Castle Line. She was converted to a troopship in 1939, returning to the Southampton-Cape Town service in 1947 and was broken up at Mihara in Japan in 1966.

rhms PATRIS
SUMMER 1972

7 DAY CRUISES TO GREECE
GREEK ISLANDS AND THE
DALMATIAN COAST

Patris (1950/18,400grt) was built as *Bloemfontein Castle* by Harland & Wolff at Belfast and sailed on her maiden voyage from London to Beira on 6 April 1950. On 8 January 1953 she went to the assistance of the Dutch liner *Klipfontein* which was sinking off Mozambique and took on board the crew and passengers. She was sold to the Chandris Line in 1959, renamed *Patris* and refitted at North Shields on the Tyne. She sailed on her first voyage for Chandris on 14 December that year from Piraeus to Sydney and operated on cruises from Australia. On 14 February 1975 she arrived at Darwin, which had been seriously damaged by a storm, and was used as an accommodation ship. She was sold in 1979 becoming *Mediterranean Island*, *Mediterranean Star* in 1981 and *Tema* in 1987 when she was broken up at Gadani Beach.

Rotherwick Castle, 1959, Union Castle Line, 9,650grt, 158m by 20m, 16½knots. She was sold to Sea Fortune Shipping Company, Monrovia, in 1975 becoming *Sea Fortune*, *Silver Rays* in 1980 and broken up at Chittagong in 1982.

Union Castle Line cargo vessels *Rowallan Castle* (1943/7,943grt) and *Roxburgh Castle* (1945/7,996grt) at Southampton in 1966. *Rowallan Castle* was broken up at Kaohsiung in 1971 and *Roxburgh Castle* in China the same year.

CLAN LINE

S.S. CLAN MACKELLAR

WILL CLOSE FOR CARGO AT

GLASGOW	BIRKENHEAD
Feb. 4th	Feb. 17th

FOR

ADEN
BOMBAY
COCHIN · TUTICORIN
MADRAS · CHITTAGONG

Intending Shippers wishing to ship Cargo by this vessel should make application for space on the appropriate form which can be obtained and lodged at any of the undermentioned Offices.

Shippers must not despatch Cargo to vessels until receipt of calling forward notice. It is essential that Shippers and Suppliers should adhere to the delivery dates shown on such notices.

Vessel has liberty to call at other U.K. Ports and at other Ports either on or out of route.
All Cargo carried by Special Agreement only and subject to all terms, conditions and exceptions of shipping notes, wharfingers' receipts and Bills of Lading
Goods insured on the most favourable Terms.
- Special accommodation for Livestock -
Freight payable in exchange for Bills of Lading.

CAYZER, IRVINE & CO., LTD.

	2 ST. MARY AXE	LONDON, E.C.3	Tel: AVE 2010
	ROYAL LIVER BUILDING	LIVERPOOL	„ Maritime 2040
	109 HOPE STREET	GLASGOW, C.2.	„ CEN 7050
BRITISH & COMMONWEALTH (AGENCIES) LTD.	MANCHESTER	„ Deansgate 7891
Do.	BIRMINGHAM	„ Midland 8271
Do.	SHEFFIELD	„ Sheffield 25880
Do.	LEEDS	„ Leeds 25790
JONES, HEARD & CO., LTD.	NEWPORT, MON.	„ Newport 64011
SIMPSON BROS. (SWANSEA) LTD.	SWANSEA	„ Swansea 50321
WM. BROWN, ATKINSON & CO. LTD.	HULL	„ CEN 36921

GLASGOW, 13th January, 1961

CLAN
LINE

...LAMONT

...RGO AT

...BIRKENHEAD
Dec. 7th

... SUEZ
...N
...MBO

...hould make application for space on ...any of the undermentioned Offices.

...calling forward notice. It is essential ...dates shown on such notices.

...ther Ports either on or out of route.
...subject to all terms, conditions
...receipts and Bills of Lading
...accepted by arrangement.
...ourable Terms.
- Special accommodation for Livestock -
Freight payable in exchange for Bills of Lading.

CAYZER, IRVINE & CO., LTD.

	2 ST. MARY AXE	LONDON, E.C.3	Tel.: AVE 2010
	ROYAL LIVER BUILDING	LIVERPOOL	„ CEN 5861
	109 HOPE STREET	GLASGOW, C.2	„ CEN 7050
BRITISH & COMMONWEALTH (AGENCIES) LTD.	MANCHESTER	„ Deansgate 7891
Do.	BIRMINGHAM	„ Midland 8271
Do.	SHEFFIELD	„ Sheffield 25880
Do.	LEEDS	„ Leeds 25790
JONES, HEARD & CO., LTD.	NEWPORT, MON.	„ Newport 64011
SIMPSON BROS. (SWANSEA) LTD.	SWANSEA	„ Swansea 50321
WM. BROWN, ATKINSON & CO. LTD.	HULL	„ CEN 36921

GLASGOW, 14th November, 1960

Clan Graham, 1962, Clan Line, 9,308grt, 155m by 19m, 16 knots. She was renamed *Candelaria* in 1981 and arrived at Kaohsiung for demolition on 23 March 1984.

Clan Maclean (1947/6,017grt) and *Clan Maclennan* (1947/6,366grt). *Clan Maclean* became *Sentosa Island* in 1976 and was broken up at Kaohsiung in 1979. *Clan Maclennan* arrived at Shanghai on 16 September 1971 for demolition.

CLAN LINE

TO
LOBITO - SOUTH & SOUTH EAST AFRICA - MAURITIUS

CAYZER, IRVINE & CO., LTD.,
LONDON - 2 ST. MARY AXE, E.C.3 - Tel. AVE 2010

Liverpool - Royal Liver Building, Tel. Maritime 2040   Glasgow - 109 Hope Street, Tel. CEN. 7050.

VESSEL	LOADS CARGO AT					Sailing B'head	DISCHARGE PORTS
	GLASGOW (King George V. Dock) Receiving	Closing	NEWPORT (Alexandra Dock) Closing	BIRKENHEAD (Vittoria Dock) Receiving	Closing		
m.v. CLAN MACDONALD	Now	21 Aug.	—	21 Aug. (For Beira)	29 Aug. Closing	2 Sep. (28th Aug.)	LAS PALMAS, DURBAN, LOURENCO MARQUES, BEIRA *
† m.v. CLAN FERGUSSON (Substituted for CLAN MACINDOE)	23 Aug.	31 Aug.	—	31 Aug. (For Beira)	8 Sep. Closing	13 Sep. (6th Sep.)	DURBAN, LOURENCO MARQUES, BEIRA *
m.v. STIRLINGSHIRE	—	—	‡ 2 Sep.	2 Sep. (For Beira)	12 Sep. Closing	16 Sep. 8th Sept.)	TENERIFFE, CAPETOWN, PORT ELIZABETH, EAST LONDON, DURBAN, LOURENCO MARQUES, BEIRA *
† s.s. CLAN MACLENNAN	31 Aug.	14 Sep.	—	14 Sep.	22 Sep.	27 Sep.	LAS PALMAS, LOBITO, WALVIS BAY, CAPETOWN, MOSSEL BAY, PORT ELIZABETH, EAST LONDON, MAURITIUS
† s.s. CLAN CHATTAN (Substituted for CLAN MACILWRAITH)	7 Sep.	21 Sep.	—	21 Sep. (For Beira)	29 Sep. Closing	4 Oct. (28th Sep.)	DURBAN, LOURENCO MARQUES, BEIRA *
† m.v. CLAN MACNAB (Substituted for CLAN DAVIDSON)	26 Sep.	2 Oct.	—	2 Oct.	10 Oct.	14 Oct.	DURBAN, LOURENCO MARQUES, BEIRA *
t.s.s. CLAN DAVIDSON (Substituted for CLAN FRASER)	21 Sep.	5 Oct.	—	5 Oct.	13 Oct.	18 Oct.	LOBITO, CAPETOWN, PT. ELIZABETH, EAST LONDON, MAURITIUS
t.s.s. CLAN URQUHART	—	—	‡ 14 Oct.	14 Oct.	24 Oct.	28 Oct.	CAPETOWN, MOSSEL BAY, PORT ELIZABETH, EAST LONDON, DURBAN, LOURENCO MARQUES, BEIRA *

‡ Subject to Inducement

* Cargo for BEIRA must be specially booked before despatch.

Through Bills of Lading issued to

| WALVIS BAY, LUDERITZ BAY | With Transhipment at CAPETOWN. | INHAMBANE, CHINDE, QUELIMANE, MACUSE, MOMA, ANTONIO ENES, MOZAMBIQUE, NACALA, PORT AMELIA. | With Transhipment at LOURENCO MARQUES |

Vessels have liberty to call at other U.K. Ports and at other ports either on or out of route.
All Cargo carried by Special Agreement only and subject to all terms, conditions and exceptions of Shipping notes, wharfingers' receipts and Bills of Lading.
† Cool Chamber and Refrigerator cargo can be accepted by arrangement.
Goods Insured on the most favourable Terms.
· Special accommodation for Livestock ·
Sailings are subject to alteration or cancellation without notice.

AGENTS

Clan Line loading notice for services from Glasgow, Newport and Birkenhead. Notice No. 11/61, 18 August 1961.

King George, 1957, Clan Line, 5,976grt, 142m by 18m, 12½ knots. She was renamed *Eleni 2* in 1972, *Taichung 2* in 1980 and broken up in Kaohsiung, where she arrived on 26 September 1982.

Clan MacIndoe, 1959, Clan Line, 7,395grt, 151m by 19m, 16 knots. She became *Gulf Heron* in 1979 and was abandoned at Basrah after being hit by shells during the Iran/Iraq war in September 1980.

Clan Robertson, 1965, Clan Line, 10,542grt, 161m by 21m, 17 knots. She was renamed *Balmoral Castle* in 1976, *Balmoral Universal* in 1979, *Psara Reefer* in 1982 and arrived at Chittagong on 19 June 1984 for breaking up.

S.A. Shipper, 1954, Safmarine, 7,878grt, 153m by 20m, 16 knots. She was built as *Clan Robertson*, renamed *Umzinto* in 1959, *Rooibok* in 1960, *South African Shipper* in 1961 and *S.A. Shipper* in 1966. She was broken up at Kaohsiung in 1975.

Clan Mactaggart, 1949, Clan Line, 8,035grt, 154m by 20m, 15 knots. She was broken up in Bilbao in 1971.

Kinnaird Castle, 1956, Clan Line, 7,681grt, 153m by 20m, 16 knots. She was built as *Clan Ross* and became *South African Scientist* in 1961, *Kinnaird Castle* in 1962, *Nazeer* in 1975 and arrived at Gadani Beach for breaking up on 26 April 1978.

Elizabeth Bowater, 1958, Bowater Steamship Co. Ltd, 4,045grt, 98m by 15m, 12 knots. She was sold in 1973 and renamed *Wimpey Sealab*, *Pholas* in 1979 and *Norskald* in 1996.

Nicolas Bowater, 1958, Bowater Steamship Co. Ltd, 7,136grt, 127m by 18m, 14 knots. She was renamed *Vall Comet* in 1974 and arrived at Karachi for breaking up on 18 October 1977.

Five

Furness Group

Newfoundland, 1948, Johnson Warren Lines, 7,438grt, 134m by 19m, 15 knots. *Newfoundland* sailed on her maiden voyage from Liverpool to St Johns, Halifax and Boston on 14 February 1948 and was sold to H.C. Sleigh in 1962 and renamed *George Anson*. She was broken up in 1971 at Kaohsiung.

Dominion Monarch (1939/26,463grt) was built by Swan Hunter & Wigham Richardson on the Tyne and sailed on her maiden voyage from Southampton to Wellington on 17 February 1939. In the following year she was converted to a troop carrier to carry 1,480 troops. She carried 90,000 troops and covered over 350,000 miles during the period of the Second World War. She was converted back to a passenger ship in 1948 and returned to service later that year. In 1962 she was employed as a floating fair at the Seattle World Fair and arrived at Osaka, Japan, on 25 November that year to be broken up.

In 1878 Christopher and Thomas Furness set up a shipping company and ordered two ships. Four years later Christopher took responsibility for the shipping line and Thomas looked after their food-handling company. Christopher bought a share in the shipyard owned by Edward Withy to build ships for his line and to sell others in the open market. The yard was taken over by the Furness brothers in 1884 and, in the following year with Thomas Wilson, they started operating the Wilson-Furness Line from Newcastle to New York.

Furness, Withy & Co. Ltd was formed in 1891, incorporating Christopher Furness & Co. and the Middleton Yard of Edward Withy & Co., Shipbuilders. The fleet consisted of eighteen vessels. The company took an interest in shipbuilding and in 1898 R.B. Stoker, a director, moved to Manchester to set up Manchester Liners.

The previous year Furness Withy started operating sailings between Manchester and Montreal and these were later expanded to New Orleans and Galveston to load cotton for the Lancashire mill trade.

The final years of the nineteenth century saw Furness Withy increase its interest in ship-building and engine building. The Gulf Line was purchased in 1903 and capital was invested in the Tyne-Tees Shipping Co.. In 1907 the ships managed by the British Maritime Trust and the Chesapeake & Ohio Steam Ship Co. were brought into the Furness, Withy fleet and the company initiated a collier service from the North East ports to London.

In 1910 the Neptune Steam Navigation Co., the Agincourt Steam Ship Co. and the Norfolk & North American Steam Navigation were taken over. A 50% share in Houlder Brothers was obtained in 1911 and the London Welsh Steam Ship Co. was purchased. A 50% share in Johnson Line was negotiated in 1914 and the Prince Line was bought in 1916. In the following

Reina Del Pacifico, 1931, Pacific Steam Navigation Co., 17,702grt, 168m by 23m, 18 knots.

year, the White Diamond Steam Ship Co. owned by George Warren was acquired. Shares were obtained in the Cairn Line in 1928 and the Gulf Line was placed into voluntary liquidation the following year.

In 1933 an interest in Shaw, Savill & Albion was acquired by the Furness Group, which increased to full control of the company in 1935. The line was established in 1858 by Robert Ewart Shaw and Walter Savill who specialized in providing shipping services to New Zealand. Competition on the route brought about its amalgamation with the Albion Line in 1882 and its involvement in the Australian trade.

The Albion Line vessel *Dunedin* carried the first cargo of frozen mutton from Port Chalmers to London in 1882 and the trade continued in partnership with the White Star Line. A holding in the Aberdeen Line was obtained in 1905. They acquired complete control of the line in 1932 and became joint owners in the Aberdeen and Commonwealth Line the following year.

The Johnson-Warren Line was established in 1934. Shares of the Royal Mail Line were obtained in 1937 and the line took over the management of the Bowater Steamship Co. in 1939.

Dominion Monarch was delivered in 1939 for the passenger service from London to New Zealand. She was the largest vessel on this route and the most powerful British motorship at the time. She was converted to a troopship and in 1942 she escaped from Singapore just before it fell to the Japanese.

Forty-two Furness Withy ships were lost in the Second World War and a programme of rebuilding took place including the entry into new trades such as ore, oil and gas carriers.

The balance of shares in the Royal Mail Line was obtained in 1965 bringing the Pacific Steam Navigation Co. into the group. PSNC was formed in 1838 with George Brown as the first Chairman. He was also one of the founders of the Royal Mail Line. The line was formed to operate coastal services from Valparaiso in Chile but later commenced operations from Liverpool to Rio de Janeiro, Montevideo and Valparaiso.

The company was acquired by the Royal Mail Line in 1910 and the opening of the Panama Canal in 1914 changed the pattern of trade to South America, proving the need for shipping lines to combine to survive. The Pacific Steam Navigation vessel *Potosi* held the distinction of being the first British ship to use the Panama Canal.

In 1922 the Chilean Government legislated to ban foreign ships from its coastal trade and the company ended its coastal shipping services which it had been operating for over eighty years. A new service was started, which operated the passenger vessels *Ebro* and *Essequibo* between New York and Valparaiso.

The new passenger liner *Reina Del Pacifico* sailed on her maiden voyage from Liverpool to La Rochelle, Vigo, Bermuda, Bahamas, Havana, Jamaica, Panama, Guayaquil, Callao, Antofagasta and Valparaiso on 9 April 1931. The following year she completed a 'Round the World' voyage and in 1936 sailed to Valparaiso from Liverpool in the record time of twenty-five days.

Reina Del Pacifico was converted to troop transport in 1939 and in that role she sailed to Norway, Suez, India, South Africa, North America, Algiers and Sicily. In 1945 she carried King Peter and the Royal Family of Yugoslavia and the United States First Division Headquarters staff to Sicily. She returned to the Liverpool to Valparaiso service in 1948 and was broken up by John Cashmore at Newport, Wales, in 1958.

Reina Del Mar was built by Harland & Wolff at Belfast in 1956 for the Liverpool to Valparaiso passenger service. However, by 1963 it was no longer viable to operate the passenger service and *Reina Del Mar* was transferred to the Travel Savings Association with the Union Castle Line managing the vessel. Union Castle eventually bought her in 1973.

Furness Ship Management was formed in 1965 to manage Furness Withy, Johnson Warren Lines, Nile Shipping, Pacific Maritime Services, Prince Line, Royal Mail Line and Welldeck Shipping. Overseas Container Line was established by Furness Withy, British & Commonwealth Shipping, Alfred Holt and the Peninsular & Oriental Steam Navigation Co.. The Shaw Savill contribution to the consortium was *Jervis Bay* which was built by Upper Clyde Shipbuilders at Glasgow. Cairn Line was taken over in 1967 and control of Houlder Brothers was obtained in 1968.

The cellular container ship *Manchester Challenge* was delivered to Manchester Liners in 1968. She was the first British built cellular container ship and was followed by three identical sisters. Ten years later container services were transferred to Liverpool and Felixstowe.

It was decided that Furness Withy should dispose of twenty-three ships in 1970 and end their Pacific Coast service. A continual decline in profits in the 1970s and a reduction in the fleet led to the group intergrating their shipping interests into one company in May 1979. In the same month Derwent was commissioned, bearing a Royal Mail name but owned by the Shaw Savill Line.

Reina Del Mar, 1956, Pacific Steam Navigation Co., 20,225grt, 183m by 24m, 18 knots.

Newfoundland, 1964, Johnson Warren Lines, 6,905grt, 131m by 19m, 16½ knots. She was transferred on charter to Shaw Savill Line and renamed *Cufric* in 1973, returned to Johnson Warren and her original name in 1974, becoming *Cufric* again in 1976. She was sold in 1978, renamed *Gaiety* and broken up in 1989.

A successful offer of 420p per share was made for the Group by C.Y. Tung's Orient Overseas Containers (Holdings) Ltd in 1980 and the Furness Withy share of Overseas Containers was bought by the other partners. The former Shaw Savill container vessel *Jervis Bay* was sold to ship-breakers in 1983, and whilst being towed to Kaohsiung, she was driven onto rocks off Bilbao, Spain and broke in two in bad weather.

Shaw Savill continued to trade in partnership with Andrew Weir & Co. Their refrigerated containership *Dunedin* provided a service between Melbourne, Sydney, Lyttleton, New Plymouth and Panama to Puerto Cabello, Port of Spain, Bridgetown, Fort France, Kingston, Vera Cruz, Houston and New Orleans. This service continued until 1984 and *Dunedin* was sold in 1986 to the German company Hamburg-Sud Amerikanische Damps.Ges. She was converted to a container ship and renamed *Monte Pascoal*.

In 1987, financial difficulties forced a restructuring of the Group with Furness Withy Shipping being retained and the sale of Furness Withy (Investments) Ltd.

However, in 1990 the last ship to be operated under the British flag by Furness Withy, the *Andes*, was registered in Hong Kong and the offshore oil business was sold to the Stena Line. Later that year Furness Withy (Shipping) Ltd was disposed of to the Hamburg-Sudamericanische Linie to become a department in that large organisation. *Andes* was renamed GCM *Magellan* in 1994, registered in the Cayman Islands and managed by Furness Withy.

Royal Mail Lines cargo and Andes Sunshine Cruise brochure, 1959.

Highland Brigade (1929/14,216grt) was the third of five sisters built by Harland & Wolff at Belfast for the Royal Mail Line's River Plate service. She was taken over by the Admiralty as a troopship during the Second World War and was returned to service in 1947. She was sold to John Latsis in 1959 and renamed *Henrietta*. In 1960 she was renamed *Marianna*, rebuilt and employed as a Pilgrim ship. She was broken up at Kaohsiung in 1965.

Aragon (1960/20,362grt) sailed on her maiden voyage from London to Buenos Aires on 29 April 1960. In 1969 she was transferred to Shaw Savill Line and renamed *Aranda* for their service to Australia. However, in 1971 she was sold to Lief Hoegh and converted to a vehicle carrier. She was sold to Ace Navigation in 1977 and renamed *Hual Traveller*, *Traveller* in 1980 and broken up in 1981.

Loch Garth, 1947, Royal Mail Line, 8,617grt, 152m by 20m, 16 knots. She was broken up at Tamise, Belgium, in 1967.

Deseado, 1942, Royal Mail Line, 9,641grt, 143m by 20m, 14 knots. She was broken up at Hamburg in 1968.

R.M.S "NOVA SCOTIA" and R.M.S "NEWFOUNDLAND"

ENJOY YOUR TRIP — GO BY SHIP.
TRAVEL BY 'FURNESS WARREN LINE'

Whether you are an ardent Sportsman, an adventurer, or just an everyday traveller looking for an ideal and refreshing change, you'll find the Furness Way to Canada and the United States, provides the answer—even to accommodating your car, if desired.

For comfortable and economical travel the "NOVA SCOTIA" & "NEWFOUNDLAND" present all the amenities for good living at sea and the limited number of passengers carried means personal service is assured.

The accommodation is of a high order both in First Class and Tourist Class, the former having Single Rooms with private shower and toilet.

Individual control of ventilation is installed in every Cabin—only one of which has no outside location.

The Public Rooms are tastefully panelled and consist of spacious Dining Saloons and comfortable Lounges with a Smoke Room and Bar in each class.

Both vessels have ample deck space for open-air recreation, deck games, etc. Cinema and Library are provided.

Year-round North Atlantic Trade

Incorporating all the latest features of stowage and the most efficient methods of ship/quay movement of cargo

● **SPEED IN HANDLING CARGO.**
By the provision of double hatches i.e. side by side, for the main cargo compartments, and a triple hatch arrangement for the No. 5 compartments, it is possible for approximately 70% of the vessel's total cargo to be placed straight into a stowed position—thus speeding up the handling of cargo. All the hatches are of the hydraulic automatic type.

● **CARE IN CARGO HANDLING.**
Additional aids to speed and care in cargo handling are the provision of carefully sited deck cranes, and the fitting of strengthened flush hatches in the tween decks to facilitate the use of fork lift trucks where necessary. The provision of these hatches also reduces the risk of damage normally associated with the manoeuvring of cargo items in the tween deck and the hull spaces of the conventional ship.

● **CARGO PROTECTION DURING VOYAGE.**
Protection of the cargo during the voyage has also received very careful attention: an efficient system of mechanical ventilation enables ten air changes per hour to be effected in all holds and tween decks.

● **CARGO CAPACITY.**
Out of the total cargo capacity of approximately 400,000 cubic feet, (bale), there is provided in five separate compartments, some 48,000 cubic feet of refrigerated space.

● **REFRIGERATION.**
Each refrigerated chamber can be controlled individually down to minus 10 degrees F., and the flooring has been specially strengthened to allow the use of mechanical handling equipment within the chambers: thus the speedy ship/quay movement essential to this type of cargo can be assured.

● **BULK LIQUID CARGO.**
Provision has been made for the carriage of bulk liquid cargoes in four tanks, with a total capacity of 450 tons. Each tank is specially coated for ease of cleaning, and has heating coils fitted.

GENERAL SPECIFICATION.

Dimensions:
Length Overall 429 feet.
Depth Moulded 34 feet 6 inches.

Tonnage:
7,300 Deadweight.

Service Speed:
16½ knots.

Classification:
Lloyds — 100 A1.

Breadth Moulded 61 feet.

Designed Trial Speed:
18 knots.

Main Engine:
Harland & Wolff/B. & W. Diesel.

The ships were designed especially for the year-round North Atlantic trade and are strengthened for navigation in ice; as can be seen from the plan they have a long forecastle to give extra buoyancy and provide the maximum degree of protection for the weather deck during periods of heavy weather. Steam lines are provided on deck for the rapid de-icing of equipment etc., during the winter months.

Furness Warren Line brochures featuring the two sets of *Nova Scotia* and *Newfoundland* sisters of 1947 and 1964.

Queen of Bermuda (1933/22,552grt) was built by Vickers Armstrong on the Tyne for the New York-Bermuda service. In 1939 she was converted to an armed merchant cruiser and was used in the South Atlantic. She was converted to a troopship in 1943. She was refitted in 1947 and returned to the Bermuda service in 1949. In her 1961/62 winter annual overhaul, she was rebuilt with one funnel but only continued in service until 1966 when she was broken up at Faslane.

Ocean Monarch (1951/13,654grt) was also built on the Tyne by Vickers Armstrong for the same service. In 1966, when the service ended, she was laid up on the River Fal until she was sold to Balkanturist at Varna in 1967, and renamed *Varna*. In 1979 she was renamed *Venus* and *Riviera*, owned by Dolphon (Hellas) Shipping, Greece. On 28 May 1981 she suffered an engine room fire at Ambelaki and was towed to sea, capsizing off Kynosoura on 1 June.

Cairngowan, 1952, Cairn Line, 7,503grt, 136m by 18m, 13 knots. She became *Manchester Engineer* in 1965, *Cairngowan* again in 1966, *Georgilis* in 1969 and was broken up at Gandia, Spain, in 1973.

Pacific Reliance, 1951, Furness Withy & Co. Ltd., 9,442grt, 153m by 19m, 15½ knots. She was broken up at Bruges in 1971.

LIVERPOOL

TO

ST. JOHN'S, Nfld., HALIFAX, N.S.

and BOSTON, U.S.A.

R.M.S. "NOVA SCOTIA"

Receiving Cargo ... ... 31st OCT. / 11th NOV.

R.M.S. "NEWFOUNDLAND"

Receiving Cargo ... ... 17th NOV. / 2nd DEC.

Loading Berth: SOUTH SIDE, HORNBY DOCK, LIVERPOOL.

THROUGH BILLS OF LADING issued to the interior of Newfoundland via St. John's Nfld., and to interior points of Canada and the U.S.A. via Halifax, N.S.

"SHIP VIA HALIFAX, N.S."

All bookings are subject to the conditions and exceptions of the Company's Bill of Lading.
The usual Customs papers Export Licences and Exchange Control Form (C.D.3), where required, MUST be in order before the goods are tendered for shipment.

REFRIGERATOR STOWAGE is available—subject to special engagement.

For Rates of Freight, Insurance and other information apply to:—

FURNESS, WITHY & CO. LTD.,

P.O. BOX 63

Royal Liver Building, Liverpool, 3.

Telephone: CENtral 9261

Telegrams:
Brantford, Liverpool, Telex
Telex No: 62441

or

FURNESS, WITHY & CO. LTD.,

GLASGOW C.1: 19 St. Vincent Place. LONDON, E.C.3: 56 Leadenhall Street.
GRANGEMOUTH: 83 Lumley Street. MIDDLESBROUGH: Lloyds Bank Chambers.
LEITH: Atlantic Chambers. NEWCASTLE-ON-TYNE: Milburn House.

HOULDER BROS. & CO. LTD.,

BIRMINGHAM, 2: Waterloo House, HULL: Daily Mail Bldgs., Jameson St.
　　　　　　　Waterloo Street. MANCHESTER, 2: 53 King Street.
BRADFORD: 69 Market Street. SHEFFIELD, 1: Norfolk Chambers,
BRISTOL, 1: 49 Queens Square. 　　　　　　　　　　　Norfolk Row.
HANLEY: Halifax Chmbs., Market Sq.

T. T. PASCOE LTD.,

CARDIFF: Crichton Hse., Mount Stuart Sq.

ALEX. M. HAMILTON & CO.,

BELFAST: 29/31 Waring Street.

R. M. BEVERIDGE & CO. LTD.,

DUNDEE: 54 Commercial Street.

Furness Warren Line notice for sailings, November/December 1960.

Rossmore (1958/206grt) and *Foylemore* (1958/208grt) carried out towing duties in the River Mersey. *Rossmore* became *Rossgarth* in 1969 and *Rozi* in 1981. She was sunk off the coast of Malta in August 1992 to create an artificial reef for divers. *Foylemore* became *Foylegarth* in 1969 and *St Budoc* in 1983.

Edenmore, 1958, Furness Withy, 10,792grt, 154m by 20m, 12 knots. She was renamed *Welcome* in 1975, *Duglasia* in 1976 and broken up at Savona where she arrived on 15 September 1983.

Reina Del Mar cruise brochure, 1972.

Salaverry, 1946, Pacific Steam Navigation Co., 6,647grt, 142m by 19m, 15 knots. She became *Pelias* in 1967 and sank near Durban on a voyage from Maceio to Saigon on 12 December 1972.

Cotopaxi, 1954, Pacific Steam Navigation Co., 8,559grt, 156m by 20m, 16 knots. She was renamed *Kavo Longos* in 1973 and broken up in China in 1975.

Somers Isle, 1959, Pacific Steam Navigation Co., 5,684grt, 121m by 16m, 14½knots. She was sold in 1971 and renamed *Eldina*, *Commencement* in 1975, and *Caribbean* and *Melpol* in 1981. On a voyage from Lisbon to Bremen she was gutted by fire which broke out on 8 December 1981 in the English Channel. She was abandoned by her crew and taken in tow to Havre, where she arrived on 10 December. She was sold to Belgium shipbreakers in 1984.

Kenuta, 1950, Pacific Steam Navigation Co., 8,494grt, 156m by 20m, 16 knots. She was broken up in Antwerp in 1971.

Southern Cross (1955/20,204grt) was launched by Her Majesty the Queen on 17 August 1954 at Harland & Wolff's yard at Belfast. She originally operated four voyages a year alongside *Dominion Monarch* and was later joined by her near sister *Northern Star*. This photograph was taken in 1971 when she was cruising from Liverpool. Later that year she was laid up in the River Fal. She was sold in 1973 and renamed *Calypso*. She became *Azure Seas* in 1980 and *Ocean Breeze* in 1993.

Northern Star (1962/24,731grt) sailed on her maiden voyage from Southampton on 10 July 1962 and joined her sister *Southern Cross* on the Round the World service. At the end of her service *Northern Star* operated a series of cruises but it was decided that she should be sold when she berthed at Southampton on her last cruise on 1 November 1975. She arrived at Kaohsiung on 11 December for breaking up.

Ocean Monarch (1957/25,585grt) was originally the Canadian Pacific liner *Empress of England*. She was sold to the Shaw Savill Line and renamed in 1970. Following her purchase she completed one voyage from Liverpool to Southampton and Australia prior to a £4 million refit by Cammell Laird at Birkenhead. She left Southampton on her first cruise for her new owners on 16 October 1971. The 1975 cruise season was shortened because of *Ocean Monarch*'s mechanical problems, and she was sold to shipbreakers at Kaohsiung, where she arrived on 17 July that year.

Majestic, 1967, Shaw Savill Line, 12,591grt, 166m by 23m, 19 knots. She became *NZ Adrangi* in 1974, *Mykonos* in 1978, *Mykonos V* in 1992 and was broken up at Alang, where she arrived on 21 March 1995.

Gothic, 1948, Shaw Savill Line, 15,911grt, 171m by 22m, 17 knots. The ship acted as a temporary Royal yacht in 1953 for Her Majesty the Queen and the Duke of Edinburgh's tour of New Zealand and Australia. She was refitted at Birkenhead by Cammell Laird and sailed from Liverpool and London to Kingston, Cristobal, Suva (Fiji), Tonga and Auckland. *Gothic* then proceded to Wellington, Bluff, Sydney, Hobart, Melbourne, Townsville, Cairns, Mackay, Adelaide and Fremantle. The Royal couple returned to Aden on Gothic and disembarked to join the new Royal Yacht Britannia at Tobruk for their return to Britain. *Gothic* gave further service to the company and was broken up in 1969.

Suevic, 1950, Shaw Savill Line, 13,587grt, 170m by 22m, 17 knots. She was broken up at Kaohsiung in 1974.

Megantic, 1962, Shaw Savill Line, 12,226grt, 164m by 22m, 18 knots. She was sold in 1979 and renamed *Dimitrios Ventouris* and arrived at Kaohsiung on 16 April 1980 for breaking up.

PRINCE LINE

REGULAR SERVICES
By Fast Modern Vessels,

MANCHESTER
(including ELLESMERE PORT)
and BELFAST, CARDIFF and BARRY (if inducement)
also ANTWERP, LONDON and EAST COAST.

MANCHESTER TO
MEDITERRANEAN

PRINCE LINE

Head Office : 56, Leadenhall Street, LONDON, E.C.3.

FORTHCOMING SAILINGS

FORTHCOMING SAILINGS
FROM
MANCHESTER

TUNIS, TRIPOLI (Libya), ALEXANDRIA,
BEYROUT and LATTAKIA.

R m.v. "NORMAN PRINCE"

Receiving Cargo :- 13th to 19th OCTOBER, 1960.

TUNIS, MALTA, ALEXANDRIA, BEYROUT,
LATTAKIA, ISKENDERUN and MERSIN.

m.v. "SCOTTISH PRINCE"

Receiving Cargo :- 27th OCT. to 3rd NOV. 1960.

MALTA, LIMASSOL, FAMAGUSTA, TEL AVIV,
and HAIFA.

m.v. "CYPRIAN PRINCE"

Receiving Cargo :- 3rd to 9th NOVEMBER, 1960.

TUNIS, MALTA, TRIPOLI (Libya), FAMAGUSTA,
ALEXANDRIA, BEYROUT and LATTAKIA.

R m.v. "HEATHMORE"

Receiving Cargo :- 16th to 23rd NOVEMBER, 1960.

No. 30. Oct. 60.

R   Refrigerator Accommodation Available.

LOADING BERTH (unless stated otherwise)
No. 6 SHED, No. 7 DOCK, SALFORD.
Vessels have the liberty to proceed to ports in any
order, and to call at other ports on or off the
advertised route

1960 Prince Line sailing list.

Merchant Prince, 1950, Prince Line, 3,343grt, 110m by 16m, 12 knots. She was built as *Sycamore* and became *Walsingham* in 1955, *Sycamore* in 1957, *Merchant Prince* in 1965, *Elias L* in 1968, *Jura* in 1973, *Meltemi* in 1975, *Temi* in 1977 and arrived at Gadani Beach for breaking up on 10 May 1979.

Pacific Stronghold, 1958, Furness Withy, 9,439grt, 153m by 19m, 15½ knots. She became *Aegis Honor* in 1971 and was broken up at Whampoa in 1974.

Southern Prince, 1956, Prince Line, 7,917grt, 142m by 19m, 14 knots. She was renamed *Medic* in 1958, *Southern Prince* in 1960, *Argosy* in 1971, *Oriental Prosperity* and *Topaz* in 1977 and arrived at Kaohsiung for breaking up on 6 March 1978.

Oakmore, 1939, Johnson Warren Lines, 4,735grt, 133m by 17m, 13 knots. She was built as *Levante* and became *Oakmore* in 1946. She arrived at Aviles to be broken up on 13 April 1967.

Manchester Faith, 1959, Manchester Liners, 4,459grt, 115m by 15m, 14½ knots. She became the *Cairnesk* in 1965, *Manchester Faith* again in 1966, *Ilkon Tak* in 1969, *Chryseis* in 1982 and arrived at Karachi on 16 October 1982 to be broken up.

Manchester Trader, 1955, Manchester Liners, 7,636grt, 142m by 19m, 14 knots. She was built as *Western Prince* and became *Zealandic* in 1957, *Manchester Trader* in 1963, *Western Prince* again in 1969 and *Mariner* in 1971. On a voyage from Havana to Kobe, she was abandoned and sank on 29 March 1973.

Manchester Challenge, 1968, Manchester Liners, 12,039grt, 161m by 19m, 19½ knots. She was renamed *Ocean Container* in 1979, *Hung Fu* in 1989, *MSC Susanna* in 1989, *Swan 1* in 1992 and was broken up at Alang in 1993.

Westbury, 1960, Houlder Brothers, 8,414grt, 139m by 19m, 13½ knots. She became *Diamondo* in 1978, *Polana* in 1981 and broken up at Gadani Beach in 1983.

Six

Harrison Line

Scholar, 1944, Harrison Line, 7,274grt, 135m by 17m, 11 knots. She was built as *Samidway* and became *Scholar* in 1947, *Konstantinos Yemelos* in 1964 and was broken up at Murosan, Japan in 1969.

Interpreter, 1948, Harrison Line, 6,815grt, 140m by 18m, 14 knots. She was renamed *Taxiarchis Michael* in 1967 and was broken up at Whampoa in 1969.

George Brown opened a ship-broking business in Liverpool in 1826 to charter steamers for the coastal and French trade. In 1839 he went into partnership with Thomas Harrison. The firm's name became George Brown & Harrison and they were initially responsible for dealing with consignments of brandy and wines which arrived at Liverpool on French sailing ships. Arrangements were made to purchase small schooners, barques and brigs including the *Lancashire*, which was built in 1853 by Bland & Chaloner.

Thomas Harrison's brother James joined the firm in 1848 and the name was changed to Brown & Harrison's. When George Brown died in 1853 the company became known as Thomas & James Harrison and they owned a fleet of sailing vessels which traded beyond French ports. *Philosopher* was their first iron ship and was built in 1857 by Thomas Vernon of Liverpool. The practice of naming vessels after trades and professions was established and this continued throughout the history of the line.

Cognac and *Gladiator* were iron-screw steamers built in 1860, and were employed in the Charente trade. *Gladiator* was sold in 1862 and became a blockade-runner during the American Civil War, surviving until 1893 when she was wrecked. *Dragon* was launched in 1861 and *Charente* the following year. Shipping operations by the company were extended to Brazil, Central America, the West Indies and India, and in 1884 the Charente Steam-Ship Co. was established to look after the steamship business. The last of their sailing ships, *Senator*, was disposed of in 1887.

Thomas Harrison died in 1888 and James in 1891. James had seen the possibilities of a canal at Suez and had several conversations with Ferdinand de Lesseps regarding its construction. Consequently, the Harrison Line chartered a number of steamers on the opening of the Canal and pioneered this route to India.

In 1904 the Harrison Line owned thirty-six steamships with a tonnage of 179,166 tons. They took over four steamers from Rathbone Brothers in 1889 and seven vessels from the Rennie Line and Aberdeen Line were merged into their fleet. Rankin Gilmour were taken over in 1918 and in 1920 Scrutton Sons & Co., Prentice Service and Henderson with eight steamers from the Crown Line were also acquired.

In 1934 most of the Leyland Line vessels went over to the Harrison ownership and by 1939 the Line owned and managed a fleet of over fifty ships including two passenger steamers, *Inanda* and *Inkosi*, which sailed between London and the West Indies.

Harrison Line lost thirty ships during the Second World War. *Dalesman* was built in 1940 and during the attack on Crete in 1941, she was engaged in taking British troops off the island. She was attacked by German bombers, and sank in Suda Bay. Her crew were taken prisoner and she was later salvaged by the Germans, renamed *Pluto*, and employed in troop carrying operations in the Mediterranean. She was attacked in Trieste harbour and sank in 1944. On completion of the War, she was rebuilt and renamed *Empire Wily* and was repurchased by Harrison Line in 1946 and renamed *Dalesman*.

In 1945 Harrison Line acquired a number of Empire and Liberty vessels to enable them to continue trading while they embarked on a rebuilding programme in British shipyards. In 1947 *Herdsman* was the first new vessel to be delivered since the end of the War and she was followed by other motor vessels as part of the extensive fleet replacement programme. The Company were renowned for providing high-quality accommodation for masters, officers and crew on their ships and the new vessels incorporated all modern aids to propulsion and navigation.

Author, 1958, Harrison Line, 8,715grt, 149m by 19m, 15 knots. She became *Humber* in 1978 and was broken up in 1979.

In 1954 Sir Thomas Harrison became vice-chairman of the Suez Canal Co., Compagnie Universelle du Canal Maritime de Suez, and in 1955 the rights of the brandy trade were sold to the Moss Hutchison Line, ending the link with the business which had originally established the Company. *Administrator* was transferred to the Bermudian registry in 1958 followed by her sister ship *Author* in 1959.

Adventurer was launched on 21 April 1959 at the yard of William Doxford & Sons Ltd at Sunderland. She was designed with her machinery aft and bridge forward to allow for the maximum cargo capacity and the carriage of long loads. She was fitted with the first Stulcken installed in a British vessel which was the heaviest of this type afloat. She was followed by near sisters: *Custodian* in 1961, *Tactician* in 1962 and *Inventor* in 1964.

In 1961 *Explorer* and *Dalesman* were the first new Harrison Line ships to be built abroad in the Netherlands and in 1964 *Discoverer*, *Statesman*, *Philosopher*, *Naturalist* and *Novelist* were built by A/B Lindholmes Varv., at Gothenburg, Sweden. They also delivered *Trader* and *Linguist* in 1966. However, in 1968 the line returned to William Doxford at Sunderland who delivered *Magician* and *Historian*. *Samaria* and *Scythia* were purchased from the Cunard Line in 1969 and were renamed *Scholar* and *Merchant* respectively. *Benefactor* entered service in 1971, with *Craftsman* following a year later.

The decision to diversify was taken in 1970 and three years later the bulk carriers *Wayfarer*, *Wanderer* and *Warrior* were built in Japan. At this time the container revolution was changing the face of British Shipping and Harrison Line joined the Hamburg America Line, KNSM and Cie Generale Maritime et Financiere in the Caribbean Overseas Line consortium. Six container vessels were ordered for the consortium from Stocznia Gdanska, Gdansk in Poland and *Astronomer* was delivered in 1977. The following year CGM joined the consortium, enabling weekly sailings to be provided. Ellerman-Harrison Container Lines provided a service to South Africa.

Author, 1980, Harrison Line, 27,867grt, 204m by 31m, 21 knots. She was renamed *Benarmin* in 1981 and *Author* in 1982.

Custodian, 1961, Harrison Line, 8,847grt, 149m by 19m, 16 knots. She became *Sea Pearl* in 1979 and *Mighty Pearl* in 1982. On a voyage from Montreal to Kingston, she went aground near Inagua Island on 2 February 1982 and was abandoned.

Wanderer, 1951, Harrison Line, 8,150grt, 140m by 18m, 12 knots. She was renamed *Cleopatra* in 1970, *Chung Thai* in 1974 and broken up that year.

Astronomer was taken over by the British Government when the Falkland Islands were invaded by Argentina in 1982 and she was renamed *Reliant*. She returned to her role as a container ship in 1987 when she was sold to the Paramatta Shipping Co. and renamed *Admirality Island*. *Advisor* was renamed GCM *Provence* in 1985.

In 1998 the Line's share in the joint Ellerman-Harrison service was sold to P&O Nedlloyd, who also acquired the Red Sea/East African liner trade in 1999 together with Barrister, which was renamed P&O Nedlloyd Djibouti. On 11 September 2000 P&O Nedlloyd announced that it had aquired the liner trading business interests of T&J Harrison for the services operated in the European to Caribbean trade and Europe to the West Coast of South America.

The Chairman of Harrison Line, Michael Seaford said that as the liner trade was becoming an environment better suited to big companies, the sale reflected a desire to concentrate on other maritime and logistic activities better suited to the company's size and structure. Harrison's would now be responsible for warehousing, transport, airfreight and distribution activities as well as supplying charts, nautical publications and navigational equipment.

Harrison Logistics was established in 2000 with the amalgamation of a number of separate shipping service companies which were acquired by Harrison Line as part of a programme of expansion into the customer sevice and forwarding sector. It was owned by Charente Ltd and took the Harrison name into the twenty-first century. However, early in 2002 it was announced that this operation would close as a victim of the recession, marking the end of an era for the Harrison Line.

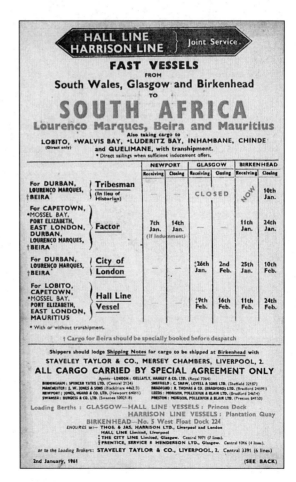

Hall Line and Harrison Line sailing list for services to South Africa in 1961.

Dalesman, 1961, Harrison Line, 7,200grt, 134m by 18m, 16 knots. She became *Adrianos* in 1979, *Ioannis* in 1981 and was broken up in 1984.

Craftsman, 1947, Harrison Line, 6,725grt, 141m by 18m, 14 knots. She was renamed *Sea Bird* in 1967 and arrived at Kaohsiung on 8 November 1967 to be broken up.

Trader, 1966, Harrison Line, 5,788grt, 127m by 18m, 17 knots. She was renamed *Bangpa-In* in 1980 and broken up at Rayond, Thailand, in 1986.

Craftsman, 1972, Harrison Line, 10,219grt, 162m by 23m, 18 knots. She became *Forum Craftsman* in 1981 and *Regal Crusader* in 1988. On 1 March 1991 she went aground in the River Parana and was refloated the following week. She was renamed Christina J in 1992 and was broken up at Cebu, in the Philippines, where she arrived on the 18 August 1994.

Seven

Vestey Group

Australia Star, 1935, Blue Star Line, 12,614grt, 165m by 21m, 17 knots. She was broken up at Faslane in 1964.

Hilary, 1931, Booth Line, 7,403grt, 129m by 17m, 14 knots. She was broken up at Inverkeithing in 1959.

In August 1897, Edmund and William Vestey established the Union Cold Storage & Ice Co. in Liverpool. They both had about twenty years' experience in the meat trade and their father, Samuel, was a Liverpool shipowner and merchant. The purpose of the business was to provide refrigerated storage for meat products and the transport of meat from Australia to the United Kingdom.

In the early years of the twentieth century, the trade in meat increased and the Vestey brothers were in negotiation with the Royal Mail Line regarding preferential freight rates for their cargoes of meat from Argentina. As the Line refused to give them any special rates they decided to charter ships to bring their products back to Britain.

They entered the shipping line market in 1909 when they purchased the *Pakeha* and *Rangatira*, which were renamed *Broderick* and *Brodmore* from the Shaw Savill Line and formed the Blue Star Line in 1911, with the Union Cold Storage as the parent holding company. A new vessel, *Brodhurst*, was delivered to the line in 1914 and by 1918 they owned nine ships. The first 'Star' vessel was built at Belfast in 1919 and was named *Royalstar* and the other ships of the fleet were renamed with 'Star' names that year.

In the 1920s they operated mainly to Argentina but also to Australia, New Zealand and the Pacific Coast of America. An order was placed for nine new ships in 1925, some of which would carry passengers, and by 1930 the fleet comprised thirty-one ships. In 1935 they took over Frederick Leyland, a Liverpool shipping company, and transferred the ownership of some of their ships to this company.

At the beginning of the Second World War in 1939, the Line owned thirty-nine ships and during hostilities they suffered many losses of ships and lives. On 30 June 1940 *Arandora Star* sailed from Liverpool to St Johns, Newfoundland with a crew of 174 and nearly 1,300 German and Italian internees with a guard of 200 men. On 2 July she was torpedoed by U-47 and sank with a loss of 805 crew and passengers.

Lamport & Holt were taken over by Frederick Leyland & Co. in 1944. They were established in 1845 when William James Lamport and George Holt set up a partnership and became ship-brokers, merchants and charterers. By 1860 they formed the Liverpool, Brazil and River Plate

Devis, 1944, Lamport & Holt Line, 9,942grt, 152m by 20m, 12½knots. She was built as *Empire Haig*, but she became *Dryden* in 1946, *Fremantle Star* in 1952, *Catalina Star* in 1956, *Devis* in 1963 and *Mondia* in 1969. She arrived at Kaohsiung on 23 December 1969 to be broken up.

Steam Navigation Co. George Holt's bother, Phillip, left the firm in 1863 to assist his other brother, Alfred Holt, in his shipping interests. They established the main trade links between Britain and Brazil and the River Plate and pioneered the Brazilian coffee trade. In 1886 a contract was obtained to carry frozen meat from the River Plate to Liverpool and by 1890 there were fifty-nine vessels in the fleet.

Sir Owen Cosby Philips, Chairman of the Royal Mail Line, gained control of the line and became chairman in 1911. Following financial problems in the Kylsant empire the line was placed in receivership in 1930 and most of the fleet were laid up. Lamport & Holt Line Ltd was formed in 1934 and their first motorship, *Delius*, was delivered in 1937.

Seventeen ships were lost during the Second World War. *Bronte* was torpedoed by U-34, south-west of Ireland on 27 October 1939 on a voyage from Liverpool to South America. *Voltaire* was converted to an armed merchant cruiser and on a voyage from Halifax to Freetown she was fired at by the German vessel, *Thor*, set on fire and sunk.

The Vestey Group gained control of the Lamport & Holt Line in 1944, and *Devis* was delivered followed by *Defoe* the following year.

The Booth Steamship Line, which dated from 1881, was purchased in 1946. The line traded between Liverpool and Leixoes, Lisbon, Barbados, Trinidad, Belem Parnaiba and Fortaleza. The company owned twenty-six ships at the start of the First World War but the decline in trade in the 1920s caused the fleet to be reduced to fifteen ships by 1930. At the beginning of the Second World War, the Booth fleet comprised nine vessels: *Anselm*, *Basil*, *Benedict*, *Boniface*, *Clement*, *Crispin*, *Dunstan*, *Hilary* and *Polycarp*. Five ships were lost by enemy action.

Hilary was joined by *Hildebrand* in 1951and *Hubert* in 1955. *Hildebrand* went aground off Cascais, near Lisbon, on 25 September 1957 and she was declared a constructive total loss. *Hilary* was broken up at Inverkeithing in 1959 and the company purchased the Belgium vessel, *Thysville*, in 1961. She was the largest vessel owned by Booth and sailed from Liverpool to South America on 16 June that year.

Amselm was transferred to the Blue Star Line in 1963 and was renamed *Iberia Star*. In 1965 she became the *Australasia*, operating on the Austasia Lines Singapore to Melbourne service.

A new passenger and cargo liner, *Argentina Star*, entered service on the Blue Star Line, London to River Plate route in June 1947. She was soon followed by three other vessels of her class: *Brasil Star*, *Paraquay Star* and *Uraquay Star*. They had a service speed of 16 knots and called at Lisbon, Madeira, Las Palmas, Teneriffe, Recife, Salvador, Rio de Janeiro, Santos, Montevideo and Buenos Aires.

One of the main features of the next ten years was the transfer of ships in the group from one company to another. In 1953 the Austasia Line was set up to provide a service between Singapore and Australia and New Zealand and Lamport & Holt took delivery of their fastest ship, *Raphael*, from Bartram & Sons at Sunderland.

In 1955 the group placed their first Blue Star Line order abroad for five vessels from Bremer Vulkan in West Germany and the New York to South America route was ended by Lamport & Holt.

With the increase in containerized cargo, the Blue Star Line formed Associated Container Transportation Ltd in 1967 with the Ben Line, Cunard and Ellerman Lines. This was to operate a container service between the United Kingdom and Australia and New Zealand. In 1975 the group set up Blue Star Ship Management to manage all the vessels in the combined fleets.

Benedict and *Boniface*, which were the last two ships to be owned by Booth Line, were delivered in 1979 and only saw seven years' service with the company. In 1986 the Booth Line operated their last sailings to North Brazil and chartered vessels to provide a service from the Lancashire port of Heysham until 1992. The Lamport & Holt name survived with the container vessel *Churchill* until 1991, when the ship was repainted in Blue Star Line colours and renamed *Argentina Star*.

Avelona Star, 1975, Blue Star Line, 9,784grt, 156m by 21m, 23 knots. She was built as *Avelona Star* and she became *Castle Peak* in 1984, *Avelona Star* again in 1988, *Hornsound* and finally *Avelona Star* in 1990.

In the mid 1990s the Blue Star Line took over the control of the Bridge Line service from Australia to Japan and Korea. On 26 January 1996 the *Pyrmont Bridge* was renamed *Australia Star*. In April 1998 P&O Nedlloyd acquired the container shipping business of the Blue Star Line for £60 million. Blue Star owned eleven ships with a total container carrying capacity of around 15,000 teus (twenty-foot equivalent units) and operated between Australia, New Zealand and North America, the Middle East and Asia. P&O Nedlloyd also took over the route between North Europe, Mediterranean and Central and South America.

However, the sale did not include the conventional refrigerated fleet which operated under the name Star Reefers by them. The Vestey Group said that the sale would enable them to focus their shipping interests on Star Reefers, the highly successful fruit carrier specializing in the movement of bananas, which was among the top five of this sector in the world. They said that the sale would further strengthen the Vestey Group enabling it to go forward debt free and with greater potential for investment in the Star Reefers business and Angliss International, the food service division.

In September 2001 it was announced that Vestey's had sold Star Reefers to Swan Reefers. The line operated with six owned and nineteen chartered vessels, which would become the world's third largest line after Lauritzen Cool and Seatrade. The Vestey Group interests were now limited to the shares they owned in Swan Reefers.

Argentina Star, 1979, Blue Star Line, 22,635grt, 207m by 29m,19 knots. She was built as *New Zealand Star*. She was renamed *Churchill* in 1986 and *Argentina Star* in 1991. She was broken up in China in April 2002.

Blue Star Line services in 1965.

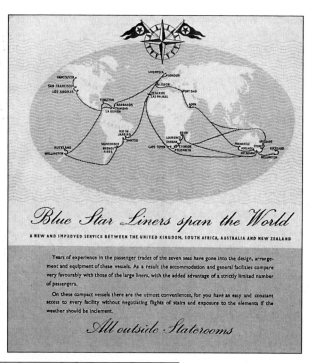

Passenger services by *Argentina Star, Brasil Star, Paraquay Star* and *Uraquay Star.*

New Zealand Star, 1967, Blue Star Line, 11,300grt, 168m by 22m, 21 knots. In 1977 she was converted to a container vessel and renamed *Wellington Star*. She was broken up at Chittagong in 1993.

Canadian Star, 1957, Blue Star Line, 6,291grt, 144m by 19m, 16 knots. She was renamed *Raeburn* in 1972 and became *Braeburn* prior to being broken up in 1979.

Townsville Star, 1957, Blue Star Line, 10,725grt, 157m by 21m, 17½knots. She was broken up at Kaohsiung in 1980.

Canberra Star, 1956, Blue Star Line, 8,398grt, 158m by 21m, 17½knots. She was renamed *Buenos Aires Star* in 1972 and broken up at Kaohsiung in 1979.

Lairdsrock (1935/471grt) and *New Zealand Star* (1935/12,436grt) berthed in Gladstone Dock, Liverpool. *New Zealand Star* was operated by Lamport & Holt Line in 1950 and the Booth Line in 1953. She was employed in the Crusader Shipping Lines service from New Zealand to Japan when she was broken up at Etajima Island in 1967.

Orwell, 1956, Blue Star Line (Managed by Gillie & Blair), 495grt, 53m by 9m, 11½ knots. She was built as *Julia Anna*, becoming *Orwell Star* in 1963 and *Orwell* in 1965. In 1968 she was sold to S. Wm. Coe & Co. Ltd., renamed *Booker Trader* and was purchased by the Booker Line in 1975. She became *Guytrader* in 1977 and *Guy Trader* in 1982.

Bernard, 1952, Booth Line, 4,459grt, 133m by 17m, 12 knots. She was built as *Siddons* and she became *Rubens* in 1955, *Bernard* in 1965, *Rossini* in 1967, *Bernard* again in 1970, *Berwell Adventure* in 1973 and *Al Turab* in 1975. She was broken up at Gadani Beach in 1978.

Ronsard, 1957, Lamport & Holt Line, 7,971grt, 144m by 19m, 17½knots. She became *Obestain* in 1980 and was broken up at Kaohsiung in 1981.

BOOTH **B** LINE

EXPRESS MAIL VESSELS

R.M.S. "DENIS"

RECEIVING
1st to 14th SEPTEMBER
AT S.W. 2 QUEENS DOCK.
SAILING FROM LIVERPOOL
15th SEPTEMBER 1960
FOR

LEIXÕES LISBON
BARBADOS TRINIDAD
BELÉM PARNAÍBA and FORTALEZA

REFRIGERATOR SPACE AVAILABLE

CARGO ALSO CARRIED ON TRANSHIPMENT BASIS TO
ANTIGUA, DOMINICA, GRENADA, MONTSERRAT, NEVIS, ST. KITTS,
ST. LUCIA, ST. VINCENT, TOBAGO, MANAUS, BOLIVIA, LETICIA,
IQUITOS and SÃO LUIS

Following vessel—R.M.S. "DUNSTAN" receiving 1st to 15th OCTOBER

For further particulars apply to:—
THE BOOTH STEAMSHIP CO. LTD., Cunard Building, Liverpool 3
Telephone No. CENtral 9181
24th August, 1960   **FOR AREA AGENTS IN U.K. SEE OVERLEAF**

Booth Line sailing list for *Denis* sailing on 15 September 1960.